START OVER,
FINISH RICH

ALSO BY DAVID BACH

Smart Women Finish Rich

Smart Couples Finish Rich

The Finish Rich Workbook

The Finish Rich Dictionary

The Automatic Millionaire

The Automatic Millionaire Workbook

Start Late, Finish Rich

The Automatic Millionaire Homeowner

Go Green, Live Rich

Fight for Your Money

PRAISE FOR *Go Green, Live Rich*

"Great news: there is no green premium! By demonstrating how going green can fit any budget, David Bach shows that good environmental and financial decisions go hand-in-hand. *Go Green, Live Rich* gives great tips, useful to everyone, about how to save money and the planet at once."

—Robert F. Kennedy, Jr.

PRAISE FOR *Smart Women Finish Rich*

"Inspires women to start planning today for a secure financial future."

—John Gray, bestselling author of
Men Are from Mars, Women Are from Venus

"David Bach is the one expert to listen to when you're intimidated by your finances. His easy-to-understand program will show you how to afford your dreams."

—Anthony Robbins, author of
Awaken the Giant Within and *Unlimited Power*

PRAISE FOR *Fight for Your Money*

"In this latest volume, Bach does not waver from his commitment to demystify the steps to financial solvency."

—*AudioFile* magazine

START OVER, FINISH RICH

*10 Steps to Get You
Back on Track in 2010*

DAVID BACH

BROADWAY BOOKS   New York

Published in the United States by Broadway Books, an imprint of the Crown Publishing Group, a division of Random House, Inc., New York.
www.crownpublishing.com

BROADWAY BOOKS and the Broadway Books colophon are trademarks of Random House, Inc.

The Automatic Millionaire Homeowner, The Automatic Millionaire, The Latte Factor, Smart Women Finish Rich, and Smart Couples Finish Rich are registered trademarks of FinishRich, Inc.

Library of Congress Cataloging-in-Publication Data
Bach, David.
 Start over, finish rich : 10 steps to get you back on track in 2010 /
David Bach. — 1st ed.
     p. cm.
 Includes index.
 1. Finance, Personal.   2. Financial crises.   3. Recessions. I. Title.

 HG179.B2444 2009
 332.024'01—dc22

 2009035406

ISBN 978-0-307-59119-7

Printed in the United States of America
10 9 8 7 6 5 4 3 2
First Edition

To Jack

I love you, buddy—
more than the earth,
the sun, and
the moon!

CONTENTS

RECOMMIT TO WEALTH

IS IT POSSIBLE TO FINISH RICH ANYMORE?

Early in the summer of 2009, I was walking down Greenwich Street in Manhattan when a woman I didn't know stepped in front of me.

"You're David Bach, aren't you?" she said.

When I admitted I was, she told me her name was Georgia and that she had read nearly all my books, starting with *Smart Women Finish Rich* more than a decade ago.

I grinned and, as I always do when I meet a reader, I asked her, "Have my books helped you?"

"Yes," she said, "a ton." But then she stopped.

"You know," she said. "I was doing great. I felt like I was finally on track and was doing everything right. But now it's all falling apart."

I asked Georgia to explain what had happened. Slowly at first, Georgia began to tell me her story. "You see, about five years ago I had nothing and I was looking to get my financial life on track. So I read your books and got going. I started 'paying myself first.' I signed up for my 401(k) plan at work. I saved 10% of my income just like you said, and I set up a college savings account for my daughter. I was really building up a nest egg, and it felt GREAT. I had nearly $70,000 in savings, plus six months' worth of expenses set aside in an emergency account. And I had *finally* paid off my credit cards. Even better, I bought a house, then rented it out and bought a second home that I live in today. And I put it all on 'automatic pilot,' like you suggested in *The Automatic Millionaire*.

"The thing is," she said, "now it feels like it was all for nothing!"

Georgia then proceeded to share a brutal list of financial woes.

As a result of the stock market slump, her 401(k) account had dropped by more than a third, along with the balance in the 529 plan she had started for her daughter's education.

At the same time, her house had declined so much in value that it was not only worth less than she had paid for it, it was barely worth what she owed on her mortgage.

To make matters worse, the guy who was renting her other house had lost his job and was way behind on the rent.

And she herself had suffered a pay cut, which forced her to dip into her security account, the balance of which was rapidly dwindling.

"I got so sick of watching my 401(k) and 529 plans lose money that I stopped saving," she added.

She shook her head sadly. "I just don't get it," she said. "Was I wrong to have saved diligently and done all those other things you advised people like me to do? I mean, where has it gotten me?"

Georgia looked up at me and sighed. *"What do I do now, David?"* she asked me. "Is it even worth it to try and start over? I've lost my motivation—and my courage."

THE SECRET TO FINISHING RICH IS, YOU CAN'T GIVE UP!

Georgia's story hit me at my core. That's because her story, or some variation of it, is shared by millions of Americans—maybe including you. Maybe you are like Georgia and you did everything right. Or maybe you never got started on the right financial road in the first place and now you're not sure if there is a point in trying. Either way, you are probably wondering if it is still possible in today's economy for someone like you—even if you don't know a lot about money, even if you don't make a lot of money—to become financially secure.

Well, I'll tell you what I told Georgia.

THE ANSWER IS YES!

Yes, you can start over (or get started in the first place!) and, yes, you can still finish rich, even in this economy. BUT you can't start over and finish rich if you give up. You have to get back up off the ground, dust yourself off, and keep going.

Recessions like the one we have just experienced are not fun. They are gut shattering, and they take a long time to recover from. But we do recover. *What's more, the aftermath of a recession is the ideal environment in which to lay the foundation for a secure, financially independent future.* Although the economy has already come a long way back from where it was in the winter of 2008–09, both real estate values and stock prices are still way below the peaks they hit in 2006 and 2007. In other words, there are bargains—in some cases, *phenomenal* bargains—to be had. More important, recessions can be a great time to reset your financial life, your goals, and your values.

DON'T GIVE UP—GET GOING! THIS IS YOUR YEAR

As I told Georgia, this is not the time to quit. This is the time to get started again. Georgia was on the right track, and the worst thing she could do would be to give up. The same goes for you. So please, for the next few hours, let's set aside the doom and gloom. Instead, let's focus on what we can do to get you back on track financially. Yes, the economy did have the equivalent of a heart attack. But don't think that means the rules for the steady, lifelong accumulation of wealth have somehow changed. They haven't. Indeed, not only do they still apply as much as they ever did, but there has never been a better time to recommit yourself to them than right now.

I'm serious about this. **I believe that the post-recession period we're in now offers a once-in-a-lifetime opportunity to build wealth and start over.** That's why I'm willing to make this promise: If you are willing to take the 10 action steps I am going to share with you in this book—starting with this first step of regaining your belief in yourself and your future—you *will* be able to start over and you *will* finish rich.

The truth is, you really don't have a choice. Like everyone else, you need to get going again. And together we can.

SOMETIMES LIFE REQUIRES YOU TO HIT THE RESET BUTTON

So listen to a little more of what I told Georgia.

I assured her that the course she had been on was the right one and that to stop saving now would be a huge mistake.

I said that when the stock market is down, you have the opportunity to buy good stocks at "fire sale" prices, and that the stocks or shares in mutual funds that she bought today could easily turn out to be the most profitable investments she ever made.

I said that real estate values go up and down and back up again, and that as long as she was able to pay her mortgage, she would continue to build wealth and independence. And if she couldn't pay her mortgage, she would still have options.

Furthermore, I pointed out that the whole point of having an emergency fund is to draw on it in an emergency, so the fact that she was doing that wasn't a bad thing. To the contrary, it meant that her financial plan was working exactly as it was intended to.

And I suggested that she was way more in control of her future than she realized.

Perhaps most important, I told her that there are as many, if not more, opportunities to build wealth during recessions and the recoveries that follow them as there are during the boom times. But you won't get anywhere if you are too scared—or feel too defeated—to do anything. *You have to have a plan based on action!*

DOING NOTHING IS THE WORST CHOICE YOU CAN MAKE

You have to hit the reset button and START OVER.

The truth is that hitting the reset button is what recessions are all about. When we go through a recession, we are all forced to "reset" how we live—what we think we want, need, and hope for. And that is often a good thing. Much of the last great boom of wealth building was built on an illusion. There was this crazy idea that it was okay to spend more than we made because our homes would always go up in value. In fact, the idea that we could always borrow on the equity in our homes to pay for stuff we didn't really need was a fantasy—a fantasy that eventually turned into a nightmare.

Now it is time to wake up and deal with the new reality. The real world is a place where we save before we spend. Where we build up our emergency accounts. Where we plan to fund our own retirement (instead of counting on the government). Where we pay down what we owe on our credit cards and our home mortgages.

It may sound boring, but when it comes to money, boring is good. In fact, it's more than good. It's ROCK SOLID, and it works.

The good news, I assured Georgia, is that despite how she might feel, she was still in charge of her life. How she handled the next few years would determine how quickly she overcame the challenges that life had thrown at her, and whether she would ultimately be stronger and smarter and richer for it.

It's in difficult times that we learn what we are made of. This is true for us both as a country and, more important, as individuals. It is always the difficult times that make us who we really are and show us who we ultimately want to be.

So I gave Georgia a hug and reminded her that her future was in her hands. She thanked me for the pep talk and promised that she would start saving again and learn to look at her house not just as a piggy bank but as a place to live and enjoy.

As I watched her walk away, I realized Georgia wasn't the only one with a new mission. I had one too. I needed to get the message out. This is *not* the time to give up.

You *can* start over. You *can* finish rich. And the time is now!

THE PROBLEM ISN'T JUST MONEY— IT'S FEAR

Standing on that Manhattan sidewalk in 2009, listening to Georgia's confusion and anxiety, I realized something very important. The biggest problem most of us are facing isn't the economy or the state of our finances. It's fear. Fear of the unknown. Fear of the future. Fear of what might happen.

True, the last few years have been a time of great economic turmoil—and that's putting it mildly. Over the course of 2008 and 2009, one of the greatest economic booms in history suddenly slammed into reverse, with disastrous results for virtually everyone. Almost before anyone knew what was happening, credit was drying up, home values were tanking, and the stock market was in a nosedive. "Not since the Great Depression" became an all-too-familiar phrase as business ground to a halt, companies laid off millions of workers, banks foreclosed on millions of homes, and much of the wealth that Americans had built up over the previous decade seemed to disappear overnight.

Their savings shrunk, their futures suddenly in doubt, tens of millions of Americans found themselves asking the same questions that Georgia was asking me. What now? Did I do it all wrong? Has the game changed? Do I keep going with my plan or do I throw in the towel? Do I wait for the market to recover and then invest again? Will real estate ever come back? Should I forget about owning a home and just rent? What about my credit cards and skyrocketing interest rates? Can I ever trust the financial companies again? Do I simply cut my spending and hope everything someday will get better?

Will I ever be able to sleep through the night again without being awakened by worries about money?

Amid all this fear and anxiety, it was easy to forget one of the most basic and important facts of economic history: Nothing goes straight up—or straight down—forever. All booms are followed by recessions, and all recessions eventually end in recoveries, often MASSIVE recoveries. We lived through an unprecedented boom time and then experienced a very difficult correction. Sure, what some people have labeled the Great Recession of 2008–09 was deeper than most, but it's behind us now and we will recover. In fact, we are already recovering. More quickly than many experts expected. As Franklin Roosevelt said back in the 1930s, the only thing we really have to fear is fear itself—fear that makes us want to pull the blankets over our heads instead of confronting the situation head-on and making sensible decisions for our future, fear that keeps us from focusing on the basics, recommitting to our financial plan, and staying positive.

ALL RECESSIONS END—ALL BUSTS LEAD TO BOOMS

If history teaches us anything, it is that all recessions end. And all busts ultimately lead to booms. Take the horrendous recession of 1981–82. That recession dragged on for 16 months, with the unemployment rate nearly reaching 11%, but it finally ended—and when it did, what followed was the longest and strongest peacetime economic expansion in the history of the United States. And the biggest rally of all followed the biggest collapse of all. In the four years following the infamous 1929 crash, Standard & Poor's 500 index fell by 83%. But after it touched bottom in June 1932, the S&P 500 soared by 132% over the next 12 months.

The human spirit—the force we all possess that drives us to live extraordinary lives, to overcome adversity and get back to having fun—is hard to deny. It is a time-tested universal truth that human beings bounce back. And when we do, we usually bounce back stronger and happier and more grounded than when we first fell down.

This happened in the Great Depression and it will happen again. We will learn once more the truth of the phrase "This too shall pass."

But this doesn't mean you can just sit back and wait for things to get better. The other great truth is that how fast you bounce back depends on how well you prepare yourself to bounce back.

This is your chance to start over and to start stronger. It is your ultimate opportunity to hit the reset button on your life, both personally and financially. Don't let it pass you by.

YOU CAN'T AFFORD TO MISS
THE NEXT GREAT RECOVERY

As I said, history has shown that deep recessions tend to be followed by historic rallies and powerful recoveries. Well, as I write this in the summer of 2009, an epic rally is roaring along like a freight train.

At the beginning of March of 2009, the stock market was in the tank. Since October 2007, when prices hit their peak, the Dow had fallen by nearly 50%, while both the S&P 500 and the NASDAQ Composite were in even worse shape (down 56% and 53%, respectively). There were real questions about the solvency of the U.S. banking system and fears that the big banks would fail, just as the giant Wall Street firm Lehman Brothers had in September 2008.

At the time, I felt strongly that the banks and financial stocks—and ultimately the market as a whole—would rally. I was right. Over the next several weeks, the banking system was fueled with government stimulus money, and the stock market and the financial-service sector staged their biggest rally in history. In less than two months (between March 9 and May 8, 2009), the Dow rose by more than 2,000 points, from 6,547 to 8,574. By the end of August, with corporate profits coming in stronger than expected and the real estate market finally showing some signs of life, the Dow had jumped to over

9,200—a 42% gain in just five months—the best six-month rally in the stock market since 1933.

Where will the market be when you read this? I don't know, but what I do believe is that by 2010 the stock market and the economy will be "resetting" and starting over. And we will all be looking at years of opportunity that none of us can afford to miss.

So the time to start over is now! With new information, updated investment strategies, and a new way of thinking and acting—all of which you will find in this book.

GO FROM SURVIVING TO THRIVING

I know you are busy, you are worried, and you want a plan that is simple. *Start Over, Finish Rich* is written with all that in mind. The START OVER ACTION PLAN to live and finish rich is designed to be read quickly and put right to work.

It is a plan designed to take you from surviving to thriving in the years to come. It is based on tried-and-true principles of building wealth based on today's market, today's economy, and our combined hope for a brighter future. It will get you back on track, it will confirm what you are doing right, and it will remind you of what you still need to do.

JOIN OUR COMMUNITY
OF SMART PEOPLE STARTING OVER

My goal with this book is to help you help yourself and others. Over the years, I have received thousands and thousands of emails and letters from readers like you who have used my books to make huge positive changes in their lives.

You can find these inspirational stories—and join our FinishRich community for free—at **www.finish rich.com**. (You can also join us on my new Facebook fan page at **www.facebook.com/DavidBach**.)

My goal is to inspire you to act. This is not the time to hesitate. This is the time to take action. What you do now will determine the kind of life you will have for years to come. You deserve the strength and power that come with positive action, and I am here to help you along the way.

As I said before, despite all the pain and upset we've been through over the last few years, the fundamental rules haven't changed. It doesn't matter what kind of beating you've taken—it's not too late to turn your financial life around and finish rich. The challenge is simple. Are you ready to put aside your fears and recommit to wealth? That's all you really need to do—just believe in yourself and follow the easy-to-understand, easy-to-do action plan outlined in this book. Like my many other readers, I hope you'll share your Start Over Success Story with me and our whole community. Send it to success@finishrich.com and let your story be an inspiration to others.

As we move from surviving to thriving in 2010 and beyond, I want you to know it is never too late to START OVER.

> Live and finish rich,
> David Bach

Take Your Start Over, Finish Rich journey to the Next Level!

MY GIFT TO YOU!

As a thank-you for reading Start Over, Finish Rich and to motivate you on your journey to recommitting to wealth, I've recorded a special Start Over video for you. Check it out at www.finishrich.com/startovervideo.

There are many ways to be part of our growing FinishRich community: Get my free newsletter, join my Facebook page, follow me on Twitter, and subscribe to my blog! Details at www.finishrich.com.

Hope to see you there!

TO DO IN 2010 ✔

- [ ] Recognize that the fundamental rules of money have not changed. Don't stop saving, don't stop investing, and don't give in to fear and despair.
- [ ] Commit to taking action on all ten Start Over steps, and start to believe again that you can live and finish rich.

FIND YOUR
MONEY

I hope the first step motivated you to get ready to start over and get going on your 2010 financial action plan. Now the question is: Where to start?

The answer: It's time to "find your money."

Every day, I talk to people just like Georgia, whom we met in Step 1. They are worried about the economy and their own financial futures. Not surprisingly, they're filled with questions. "Is this a good time to invest in real estate?" they ask me. "What do you think about foreclosure properties?" "Should I buy mutual funds or individual stocks?" "What's the best way to get back all the money I lost in my 401(k)?"

These are all good questions, but for most people

they are the WRONG questions to ask first. That's because for most people—and maybe this includes you—there's one question that has to be answered BEFORE they can start dealing with all those other issues. And that is this:

**Where is your money now
and where does it go every day?**

Do *you* know?

Here's the deal in a nutshell: If you don't know where your money is—and where your money is going—you can't start over financially. First you have to find your money. Then you can make a plan.

YOU HAVE TO FACE THE FACTS OF WHAT YOU HAVE AND DON'T HAVE

Back in the winter of 2008–09, when the stock market was hitting bottom, a lot of people simply couldn't bear to watch what was happening to their savings and retirement accounts. So they stopped looking. I guess that's understandable, but when it comes to money, ignorance is definitely *not* bliss.

Getting your finances organized—understanding where your money is and where it is going—is the key to starting over. In order to make a financial plan that is based on reality (as opposed to wishful thinking), you need to do two things:

1. Determine what all your assets and obligations are.
2. Figure out where you spend your money, month by month, day by day.

In this step, I'm going to share with you how to do both of those things. First, I'll show you how to get organized with my painless "Start Over" File Folder System. Then I'll help you get a handle on your spending by figuring out your Latte Factor. Are you ready?

Then let's get started!

ALL YOUR BILLS IN A BOX— THE "START OVER" FILE FOLDER SYSTEM FOR 2010

Let's face it—organizing your finances can be a real chore. Every month, you get sent dozens of statements, bills, and other financial documents in the mail and online. It can be overwhelming. The good news is that there's a way to get organized that's amazingly easy and relatively painless—a system that allows you to find your bills and important documents quickly and without worry.

I first developed my file folder system back in the 1990s, and it's one of the top things my readers thank me for. That's probably because it is one of the few things you can do in less than an hour at home to fix and secure your financial life. Many people—maybe you're one of them—waste literally hundreds and sometimes thousands of dollars a year paying late fees, interest fees, and penalty fees because they can't find their bills in a pile of other financial "stuff" and, as a result, miss their payment deadlines.

Of course, times change and our needs change with them. So I have taken the FinishRich File Folder system that I've described in my previous books and updated it for the current economic environment. What hasn't changed is that it is still simple and you can still set it up at home in less than an hour.

Here's what you do: First, get yourself 15 or so hanging folders and a box of at least 50 file folders to put inside them. Then label the hanging folders as follows:

THE FINISHRICH FILE FOLDER SYSTEM

☐ 1. "Tax Returns." This hanging folder should contain four file folders, one for each of the last three years plus one for the current year. Mark the year on each folder's tab and put into it all of that year's important tax documents, such as W-2 forms, 1099s, receipts to support deductions or credits, and (most important) a copy of all the tax returns you filed for that year. Generally speaking, you don't need to keep tax records for more than three years, although some documents—such as records relating to a home purchase or sale, stock transactions, retirement accounts, and business or rental property—should be kept longer. I keep all my tax documents for at least seven years, but that's an individual decision.

☐ 2. **"Retirement Accounts."** All of your retirement-account statements go here. You should create a file for each retirement account that you and your partner have. If you have three IRAs and a 401(k) plan, then you should have a separate file for each. The most important documents to file are the quarterly statements. If you have a company retirement account, you should also definitely keep your sign-up package, because it lists the investment options you have—something you should review at least once a year. You *don't* need to keep the prospectuses that the mutual-fund companies mail you each quarter.

☐ 3. **"Social Security."** Keep your most recent Social Security Benefits Statement in this folder. If you haven't received a statement in the mail in the last 12 months, request one by going online to **www.ssa.gov** or telephoning the Social Security Administration toll-free at (800) 772–1213.

☐ 4. **"Investment Accounts."** This folder is for every statement you receive related to any investments you may have (mutual funds, stocks, bonds, etc.) that are *not* in a retirement account. Prepare a separate file folder for every brokerage account you maintain.

☐ 5. **"Savings and Checking Accounts."** Keep your monthly bank statements here, with a separate file folder for each account. Generally speaking, you don't need to keep bank statements for more than a few months—certainly not more than a year. If you get your statement online, print out a copy and stick it in the file.

☐ 6. **"Household Accounts."** If you own your own home, this hanging folder should contain the following files:

"House Title," for documents such as title reports and title insurance policies. (If you can't find this stuff, call your real estate agent or title company.)

"Home Improvements," for all your receipts for any home-improvement work you do. (Since home-improvement expenses can be added to the cost basis of your house when you sell it, which means a bigger tax deduction for you, you should keep these receipts for as long as you own your house.)

"Home Mortgage," for all your mortgage statements. (Which you should check regularly, since mortgage companies often *don't credit you properly.*)

If you're a renter, this folder should contain your

lease, the receipt for your security deposit, and the receipts or canceled checks for your rental payments.

☐ 7. **"Credit Card DEBT."** Make sure you capitalize the word "DEBT" so it stands out and bothers you every time you see it. I'm not kidding. In my view, credit card debt is the biggest problem facing American consumers today. In Step 3, I will lay out a detailed plan for how you can pay down your debt as responsibly and quickly as possible. Right now simply create the folders—a separate one for each credit account you have—and keep your monthly statements in them.

☐ 8. **"DOLP™ Worksheet."** DOLP stands for "Dead On Last Payment." This is the system for paying down debt that I have taught for nearly a decade. I will explain exactly how it works in Step 3. In the meantime, make a copy of the DOLP worksheet on page 44 and put it in this file. (You can also download the worksheet from **www.finishrich.com/DOLP**.)

☐ 9. **"Credit Scores."** This folder is for your most recent credit scores, along with the credit reports on which they are based. See Step 4 for details on what these are and how to get copies.

☐ 10. **"Other Liabilities."** This is where you keep all your records dealing with debts other than your

mortgage and your credit card accounts. These
would include college loans, car loans, personal
loans, etc. Each debt should have its own file folder,
which should contain the loan note and your payment records.

☐ 11. "Insurance." Make separate file folders for
each of your insurance policies, including health,
life, automobile, homeowner's or renter's, disabil-
ity, long-term care, and so on. Each of these folders
should contain the appropriate policy and all the
related payment records. If you have any employer-
provided insurance (e.g., medical coverage), include all the brochures and other informational
material you've received from your company.

☐ 12. "Family Will or Trust." This should hold a
copy of your most recent will or living trust, along
with the business card of the attorney who drafted it.

☐ 13. "Children's Accounts." If you have children,
create a folder for all statements and other records
pertaining to college savings accounts and any other
investments you may have made on their behalf.

☐ 14. "Latte Factor®." Here is where you keep your
Latte Factor worksheet. For some of you, this may be
the most important folder you create.

NOW YOU ARE
ORGANIZED FINANCIALLY

You did it. You now have 14 hanging files (13, if you don't have kids), organized in a box or a file cabinet that represents your entire financial life. You should already be feeling more empowered and more in control over your finances. In fact, you are. In getting your records organized, you have taken a major step toward getting your financial life back on track.

I'm not exaggerating when I say that this one exercise can have a huge impact on your life. Over the years, I have heard from countless readers who told me that simply setting up this filing system totally changed how they handled their finances. It has helped couples get on the same page and stop fighting about money. It has helped people who never had a plan get a plan. Please trust me and do this. You will feel better and it will only take an hour. So go do it now.

As you create your file folder system, you may find that you don't have any documents to put in some of the folders. Make them anyway. If you don't have, say, a will or living trust, the empty folder will remind you every time you open the file box or drawer that you still have "homework" to complete for your "Start Over" plan.

If you are missing documents, use the form below to list what is missing and what you need to do to fill in the gaps.

MISSING INFORMATION	DUE DATE	COMPLETED ✔
1. _____		☐
2. _____		☐
3. _____		☐
4. _____		☐
5. _____		☐
6. _____		☐

Fill in the "Due Date" so you have a specific goal and time frame to meet. Check off "Completed" when you're done.

WHICH RECORDS SHOULD YOU KEEP AND WHICH CAN YOU DITCH?

The reason I made the FinishRich File Folder System so specific is that many of us keep too much information for way too long. (I'm guilty of this myself.) The fact is, except in cases involving fraud, the statute of limitations on income-tax returns is only three years, so the Internal Revenue Service does not expect you to hang on to tax records and receipts for any longer than that. The main exceptions to this are if you've underreported your income (in which case you should keep your records for six years) or have claimed a loss from worthless securities (seven years).

Obviously, you should keep records documenting the cost basis of your home and all your other taxable investments for as long as you own them. The same goes for the basic documents concerning your retirement accounts and insurance policies, not to mention all loans and mortgages.

But don't be shy about getting rid of old materials. Here's a list of items you should consider throwing away (or shredding if the documents contain personal information):

- Outdated warranties
- Outdated instruction manuals
- Outdated wills or trusts (provided you created a new one)
- Canceled insurance policies
- Credit card statements for closed tax years
- Canceled checks for closed tax years
- Old brokerage statements for closed tax years (unless they have cost-basis information you might eventually need)
- Old annual reports from stocks and/or mutual funds
- Old investment newsletters (some people keep these things for years because they paid for them—let them go)

ORGANIZE YOUR FINANCIAL LIFE ONLINE

Setting up and maintaining the "Start Over" File Folder System is extremely easy. Nonetheless, all that filing and storing of actual paper documents may strike some people as incredibly old-fashioned. If you're one of those people, don't worry. There is an entire new generation of extremely cool websites armed with powerful digital tools to help you track and manage your finances online. As one of these websites puts it, "We download, categorize, and graph all of your finances **automatically** every day. Know where you're spending, without spending any effort."

Is that cool or what?

Many of these sites are FREE. Two of the best are **www.mint.com** and www.wesabe.com. Both offer personal budgeting tools that allow you to track your cash flow, checking and savings accounts, credit cards, loans, and investments—all in one place. They can also analyze your spending, helping you to identify where you can cut back. Mint.com will even send you email alerts to keep you from getting hit with penalty fees for late payments, going over your credit limit, and dropping below a minimum-balance requirement.

NOW THAT YOU KNOW WHERE YOUR MONEY IS, FIND OUT WHERE IT GOES

Okay—you've got yourself organized. You know where your money is, what you have, and what you owe. Now comes the real challenge—getting a handle on your spending. You have to really work to keep what you work so hard to earn. Luckily, there's an easy, fun way to do that. You have to find what I have termed **The Latte Factor®**.

If you take only one piece of advice from this book, take this one. Even if you don't do anything else, simply finding your Latte Factor will make you financially stronger than you have ever been and stronger than almost everyone you know.

And thanks to the Internet and digital technology, finding your Latte Factor is easier today than it has ever been.

FIND YOUR LATTE FACTOR
AND FIX IT—NOW AND FOREVER!

Chances are that you have already heard about the *Latte Factor*. If you Google it, nearly 200,000 hits come up. It's a phrase that has become synonymous with saving money by cutting out small expenses. But it is more than that. At its core, the Latte Factor is the ultimate metaphor for how we spend money. It shows us the way small amounts we spend daily, on little things like fancy coffees and bottled water, can literally add up to a fortune. It is NOT about giving up your favorite cup of morning coffee at your favorite coffee shop. It's about considering where your money really goes and asking yourself, "Is this spending really worth it? What else could this money be doing for me?"

I first came up with the concept back in the early 1990s when I was teaching an investment course in California. During my class one evening, a young woman named Kim raised her hand and announced she couldn't save any money because she was living paycheck to paycheck. At the time, she was sipping a latte from Starbucks.

I responded by asking her to walk me through every single purchase she made in the course of a typical day.

As Kim told it, her spending day started on her way to work with a stop at Starbucks, where she bought herself a double nonfat latte ($3.50) and muffin ($1.50). Her next purchases came during her 10 A.M. coffee break: a fruit smoothie ($3.95) with a high-protein "juice boost" (50 cents), plus a power bar ($1.75).

I stopped her at that point and wrote the following on the blackboard:

Double nonfat latte	$3.50
Nonfat muffin	$1.50
Fruit smoothie	$3.95
"Juice Boost"	0.50
Power bar	$1.75
	$11.20

"So we're not even at lunch yet," I said, "and you've already spent more than 10 dollars. And you haven't even had any real food."

Everyone in the class broke up laughing— including Kim.

"You know we're not trying to make fun of you," I said. "The only reason everyone is laughing is that we all know we're just as bad with our money as you are. We may not like to admit it, but we all spend small amounts of money every day and never think of what it adds up to. But let me show you something that I think will amaze you."

I pulled out my calculator. "Let's say, for the sake of argument, that today, this very day, you started to save money. I'm not saying you cut out all your spending—just that you reduced it a little. Let's say you realized you could save five dollars a day and, instead of spending it on another latte, you put it in your 401(k) account. Does that sound like something you could do? Just five dollars a day, okay?"

Kim nodded.

I asked Kim her age (she was 23) and punched a bunch of numbers into my calculator. Saving $5 a day would net her $150 a month, or almost $2,000 a year. So how much did Kim think she would have in her 401(k) by the time she was 65?

She had no idea. "Maybe $100,000?" she guessed.

In fact, the answer is many, many times that

amount. Back in the early 1990s, it was reasonable to assume she could earn a 10% annual return on her money over the next 42 years—which would have left her with a nest egg of nearly *$1.2 million*. That may seem unrealistic these days, but even taking into account the recent stock market meltdown, the fact is that over the *past* 42 years (from May 1967 through April 2009) the S&P 500 has generated an average annual return of 8.76%. At this rate, Kim's $5-a-day savings would balloon over the next 42 years into $782,647!

And that's not counting the impact of the matching contributions that most U.S companies make to employees' 401(k) accounts. As I told Kim, if her company matched just 50% of what she put in (which is what most companies still do today), she'd actually be saving close to $3,000 a year. And even with today's lower rates of return, Kim would still have well over a million dollars in her account by the time she hit 65.

WHAT IF I DON'T DRINK COFFEE?

Whenever I talk about the Latte Factor, someone always objects that they don't drink coffee and would never waste the money Kim did buying nonfat muffins and power bars. But that misses the point. What we're talking about here isn't just lattes. What we're talking about is that we don't realize how much we spend on little things and how, if we thought about it and changed our habits just a little, we could change our destiny.

Take cigarettes. They aren't just a health risk; they are also a financial risk. In New York City, where I live, cigarettes are taxed so heavily that a pack now costs nearly $11. Yet hundreds of thousands of people—particularly young adults—buy them every day.

How much money literally goes up in smoke this way? Here are the figures.

A PACK OF CIGARETTES A DAY KEEPS RETIREMENT AWAY

A pack a day = $11

A pack a day for a month = $330

A pack a day for a year = $4,015

A pack a day for a decade = $40,015

The point is that whether you waste money on fancy coffee, bottled water, dining out, cigarettes, soft drinks, candy bars, fast food, whatever it happens to be—we all have a Latte Factor. We all throw away too much of our hard-earned money on unnecessary "little" expenditures without realizing how much they can add up to. The sooner you figure out your Latte Factor—that is, identify those unnecessary expenditures—the sooner you can start eliminating them. And the sooner you do that, the more extra money you'll be able to put aside. And the more extra money you can put aside, the stronger your financial position will be.

USE THE POWER
OF THE LATTE FACTOR

If you invested $10 a day (or $300/month) and earned a 10% annual return, you'd wind up with:

$$
\begin{aligned}
1 \text{ year} &= \$3,770 \\
2 \text{ years} &= \$7,934 \\
5 \text{ years} &= \$23,231 \\
10 \text{ years} &= \$61,453 \\
15 \text{ years} &= \$124,341 \\
30 \text{ years} &= \$678,146 \\
40 \text{ years} &= \$1,897,224
\end{aligned}
$$

TAKE THE "START OVER"
LATTE FACTOR CHALLENGE

On the next page is a form I call THE "START OVER" LATTE FACTOR CHALLENGE. What I want you to do is make a copy and carry it with you everywhere for the next seven days, using the worksheet to track every dime you spend. Don't change anything about your behavior. Simply spend money the way you always do. The only thing that you should do differently is to make sure you record all your spending on the form.

If you are married or in a committed relationship, get your partner to take the Challenge along with you. You can also enlist your kids or your friends. To download more of these worksheets, visit our website at **www.finishrich.com** and click on "Latte Factor Challenge."

THE "START OVER" LATTE FACTOR CHALLENGE		
DAY _____		DATE _____
Item: What I Bought	Cost: What I Spent	Wasted Money? (✔ for Yes)
1		
2		
3		
4		
5		
6		
7		
8		
9		
10		
11		
12		
13		
14		
15		
My Latte Factor Total (Total Cost of Checked Items):		

You will be amazed how quickly you get into it. The fact is, it can be mind-boggling to learn where your money goes. If you have done this before, I strongly suggest you do it again. The fact is that your Latte Factor is constantly changing, and you will find new expenses you didn't have the last time you went through this exercise.

GO HIGH TECH—
THREE MORE WAYS
TO TRACK YOUR LATTE FACTOR

Using the worksheet to track your spending is the old-school method. For those of you who prefer the high-tech route, you've got three easy options:

1. Sign up (for free!) to use my new web-based Latte Factor calculator, available at **www.thelatte-factor.com**. In addition to helping you track your spending, it also calculates what you could potentially save by cutting back on needless expenses. While you're visiting the Latte Factor website, you can also get a little inspiration by checking out all the success stories posted by readers just like you who simply didn't believe they could reduce their spending . . . until they took the Challenge. (You can also post your own story and enter the contest we have to win a free Latte Factor mug or similar prize.)

2. Access the Latte Factor calculator on my Facebook page at **www.facebook.com/DavidBach**. It works just like the calculator on our website. And you can join others who are sharing what they have saved and how it has changed their lives.

3. If you have an iPhone, download my new Latte Factor iPhone application. You can get it at the iTunes store. Just like the calculator, this app is easy to use and will help you automatically track where your money is going and how much you might be saving.

NOW GO DO IT

At this point, I would like you to stop reading and do one of three things: make a copy of the "Start Over" Latte Factor Challenge form on page 34, register to use the Latte Factor calculator on my website or Facebook page, or download the Latte Factor iPhone app.

I'm serious. Stop reading and do this now.

Getting a handle on your spending is the start of starting over. It's definitely NOT something you can afford to put off.

WHAT IS YOUR LATTE FACTOR?

Over the years, I have received thousands and thousands of emails and letters and thank-you cards from people who have used the Latte Factor—and the Latte Factor Challenge—to change their lives by changing how they think about spending money and how they really spend it. Some saved $5 a day by brown-bagging a sandwich from home instead of buying one at work. Others saved hundreds of dollars a month by giving up cabs for buses, dropping their premium cable channels, and forgoing regular manicures and massages.

Everybody's spending habits are different, and so are everyone's solutions. What we all have in common is that every one of us is capable of cutting back.

Below, fill in the first three blanks, then go to **www.thelattefactor.com** and use the calculator there to see how much your Latte Factor is costing you.

My Latte Factor is _____.

My Latte Factor is costing me $ _____ a day.

$ _____ a month.

$ _____ a year.

Over 30 years (use the calculator), at _____ % my Latte Factor is costing me $ _____.

WELL DONE!

In the pages to come, I am going to challenge you to put aside money to pay down your debt, save for your retirement, build up your rainy-day fund, and more. I can hear your reaction now. "David," you are going to ask, "where on earth do you expect me to find the money to do that?" Well, here's my answer. Just pull out your Latte Factor Worksheet. It's the kick start to your "Start Over" plan.

If you truly do this one step, your financial life will be on a better track than it may ever have been on before. You will have organized your finances at home and you will have a better understanding of where your money really goes. You'll be ready to deal with the monster that is strangling all too many Americans—credit card debt.

TO DO IN 2010 ✔

☐ Organize your financial records using the "Start Over" File Folder System. This will show you what you have and what you owe. Throw away or shred your outdated documents.

☐ Track your spending for seven days using the Latte Factor Challenge worksheet. How much daily savings can you find? Remember that even $5 a day means more than a million dollars at retirement.

DEAL WITH YOUR CREDIT CARD DEBT

If you don't have credit card debt, congratulations! You can move on to Step 4. But if you are like millions of Americans, the past year may have pushed your debt situation from not-great to red alert. As the economy got tight, the credit card companies have increased interest rates, lowered credit ceilings, and canceled accounts in an attempt to shore up their bottom line. Even before the recession made them more creative, their schemes worked so well that American consumers currently owe nearly $1 trillion in credit card debt—and are paying an additional $15 billion or so each year in fees they don't deserve.

If you are among the millions of Americans who are drowning in credit card debt (and some experts estimate this group may include as many as 50 million of us), there are two things you should know— you are not alone and you truly can fix this problem. It won't be easy, but you *can* get out of debt. In fact, you can probably do it without any outside help!

This chapter will provide you with a road map to get you back on a solid financial footing once and for all. In the next few pages I will teach you what I call my DOLP® system. DOLP stands for Dead on Last Payment. It's a simple, proven way to prioritize your debts and figure out in literally minutes how to pay them off as quickly and efficiently as possible. I'm also going to share with you how the new credit card laws enacted in 2009 can protect you from the credit card companies that helped you get in this mess in the first place.

AREYOU IN CREDIT CARD DEBT? HOW DID YOU GET THERE?

According to Federal Reserve statistics, the average family that carries a credit card balance owes nearly $17,000. That's the average. In my experience as a "money coach" for nearly two decades, I've seen firsthand that when it comes to credit cards, many of us operate way, *way* above the average. On *Oprah*'s Debt Diet Series and on the weekly "Money 911" segments I did on the *Today* show in 2009, I met people who had $25,000, $50,000, $75,000—even more than $100,000—in credit card debt.

The amazing thing about this is that credit cards don't have arms or legs. They can't jump out of your wallet or your purse and go on a spending spree on their own. So if you are over your head in credit card debt, how exactly did you get there? Be honest. Did you buy things you wanted or things you needed? Did you live beyond your means? Or did you run into a crisis, like having to pay for an expensive medical problem or feeding your family after you lost your job?

Everyone's situation is different. But there is one thing I can tell you that I know is true: Whatever got you into credit card debt is going to keep you there *if you don't change how you spend money.* My grandmother used to say, "If you can't pay cash, you can't afford to buy it." So if you are drowning in debt, my best advice is this: STOP USING YOUR CREDIT CARDS. Once you are in a hole, YOU MUST STOP DIGGING.

IF YOU'RE ABLE TO MAKE THE MINIMUM PAYMENT ON YOUR CREDIT CARD DEBT, HERE'S WHAT YOU SHOULD DO

Okay—you've accepted your share of responsibility for your problem and you've put your credit cards away. Now it's time to start reducing that mountain of debt you somehow managed to run up. The first big question you need to answer is whether you can afford to make the minimum payments on all your credit card accounts. If the answer is yes, then you can—and should—immediately start using my DOLP® debt-reduction system. If the answer is no, then DOLP won't work for you, but later on in this chapter I'll have some other suggestions that will.

As I said earlier, DOLP stands for Dead on Last Payment—and it is meant to solve a problem that trips up most people who owe credit card debt. Generally speaking, people in real debt trouble owe money on more than one credit card. Often, there can be as many as a half-dozen accounts with balances due. So how do you handle that? Should you pay a little on all of them each month or concentrate on trying to pay off just one? And if so, which one?

Without a coherent plan of attack for paying off your debt, you really don't have a chance. The DOLP system is designed to give you that plan of attack by prioritizing your debts—that is, establishing the order in which you should pay down your various cards.

Are you ready? This will take no more than 10 minutes.

DOLPING YOUR WAY OUT OF DEBT

1. Pull out your credit card statements and get them organized. Make file folders for all your credit accounts. Ideally, the folders should be red so they will stand out in your file drawer. On the front of each, use a big black marker to write the total amount you owe on that card. The point of all this is to get your debts organized. Having bills lying around your kitchen in a bowl, or in a drawer, or on top of the television, is not a system. So put down this book, go get the files, and start labeling them.

2. Get yourself a DOLP worksheet and fill it out. You'll find a blank worksheet on page 44. You can tear it out, photocopy it, or download and print out a copy for free from **www.finishrich.com/dolp**. Whether you do it by hand or use the interactive tool on the website, filling out the worksheet is really easy. You simply write in the name of the account, the outstanding balance you owe, the minimum monthly payment, and the payment due date. (For now, don't worry about the DOLP number and the DOLP ranking.)

3. Calculate each account's DOLP number. Give each account its own DOLP number. You calculate it by dividing the outstanding balance by the minimum monthly payment. For example, say you owe $1,000 on your Visa card and the minimum monthly payment is $50. Dividing $1,000 by $50 gives you a DOLP number of 20. Do this for all of your credit card accounts.

DOLP WORKSHEET

Account	Outstanding Balance	Minimum Monthly Payment	Payment Due Date	DOLP Number (Balance ÷ Min Payment)	DOLP Ranking

4. Assign a DOLP ranking to each account. The account with the lowest DOLP number is ranked #1. The account with the second-lowest number is #2. And so on. The table on page 45 gives you an example of how this might look.

5. Calendar the due dates. Enter the payment due dates for all your credit accounts in your computer's calendar system. Set your calendar software to remind you of each due date at least five days in advance so you don't make any late payments and add to your misery by getting hit with costly late fees and penalties. And sign up for those email alerts the credit card companies will send you when your bills are coming due.

DOLP WORKSHEET

Account	Outstanding Balance	Minimum Monthly Payment	Payment Due Date	DOLP Number (Balance ÷ Min Payment)	DOLP Ranking
Visa	$500	$50	10th of the month	10	1
Master-Card	$775	$65	15th of the month	12	2
Sears Card	$1,150	$35	1st of the month	39	3

6. Start paying down your debt—the DOLP way.
Each month, as the payment due dates approach, make the minimum payment on every account . . . EXCEPT for the one with the #1 DOLP ranking. For that card, make as big a payment as you can manage. Ideally, your payment should be at least double the minimum. (Hopefully, finding your Latte Factor will make it easier to come up with the extra money you will need for this.) Using the examples in the sample worksheet, you would pay $65 to MasterCard, $35 to Sears, and at least $100 to Visa. Once a card has been paid off entirely, you retire it and start paying down the card with the #2 DOLP ranking—in the example above, the MasterCard.

YOU NOW HAVE
A SYSTEM TO FREE YOU FROM
CREDIT CARD DEBT

The DOLP system works by identifying the card you can pay off most quickly and then having you pay it off first. The point of doing this is to reduce the number of different cards you owe money on as fast as possible.

This is super important, because the more balances you carry, the greater the chance that you will miss a payment or go over a credit limit—and get hit with a huge penalty. The fact is, a card with even a small balance can cost you a fortune. If you miss a payment on an account with a $500 balance, the late fee could be as much as $50. If you exceed your credit limit at the same time, the fee could be $100. This is why credit cards with small balances are as dangerous as big ones.

HOW TO GET
YOUR INTEREST RATES
LOWERED

You can make your DOLP plan work even faster by lowering the interest rates on your cards. As I write this in the summer of 2009, the average fixed rate for standard cards is 13.46%, but the rate you are being charged is likely much higher than that. Many of you have credit cards that charge rates approaching 30%.

Unfortunately, the interest rate game is one for which there is no clear road map. It used to be that to get the credit card company to lower your rate, all you had to do was ask. These days, it is a different story entirely. Indeed, some companies have been known to respond to customers' requests for lower rates by jacking them up!

Here's the approach I'd suggest for getting a better interest rate in this era of tight credit.

First, know the rate you are currently paying on each of your cards. You should find a listing for "annual percentage rate" (or APR) at the bottom of your most recent credit card statement.

Second, find out how your rates compare to the national averages. You can get the latest averages at websites like www.bankrate.com, www.lowcards. com, www.cardtrak.com, www.creditcard.com, www. cardweb.com, and www.credit.com.

The credit card companies offer five basic kinds of rates, depending on what kind of borrower they're dealing with: super-prime for the most creditworthy, prime for average borrowers, sub-prime for below-average types, promotional for new customers, and punitive for those who've broken the rules (say, by missing payments or exceeding their credit limits). The following table shows how the rates differ for each category.

FIVE KINDS OF CREDIT CARD RATES

	JULY 09	JANUARY 09	JULY 08
SUPER-PRIME	7.55%	9.00%	9.88%
PRIME	12.05%	13.37%	14.17%
SUB-PRIME	18.99%	19.49%	21.33%
PROMOTIONAL	2.01%	1.68%	2.32%
PUNITIVE	27.75%	28.57%	29.99%

Note: Average rates based on FICO credit scores.
Super-Prime = 760–850; Prime = 660–759; Sub-Prime = 500–659.
Source: CardTrak.com

When you compare your rates to the current averages, make sure you are in the right category. A "super-prime" borrower shouldn't be paying a regular "prime" rate. If you are, call your credit card company and ask why. Remember, unless you make a little fuss, no one is going to help you.

When you call the card company, USE YOUR KNOWLEDGE. Don't settle for the first person who happens to pick up the phone. Always ask to speak to a supervisor. Once you get one (and you may have to insist, since some credit card companies now train their customer-service people NOT to transfer your call), go over your rate, compare it to the competition's, and ask whether they would be willing to work with you to give you a better deal.

If the answer is: "Sorry, but there is nothing we

can do," ask them how is that possible? The fact is, there is *always* something they can do. The card companies lower their rates all the time, every day of the year, every minute of the day. On the Oprah Debt Diet, I worked with one couple who had 12 credit cards, and we were able to get all but one of them to lower their rates to below 5%. In some cases, it took multiple calls, but it paid off in the end.

TRY THE CREDIT CARD COMPANIES' DEDICATED HELP LINES TO GET YOUR RATE LOWERED

Each of the major credit card companies has a dedicated help line devoted exclusively to assisting customers who are having problems with credit card debt. If calling the company directly does not get you a lower interest rate, the folks on the dedicated help line may be able to do better.

Here are the key phone numbers. (You can also find them on **www.helpwithmycredit.org**, which I will discuss in a second.)

1. Bank of America: (800) 500-5306
2. Capital One: (866) 929-5303
3. Discover Card: (866) 567-1660
4. FIA Card Services: (888) 635-0776

5. Citi: (866) 936-4814
6. Citi, for your Sears Card®: (866) 532-9532
7. Citi, for The Home Depot® Credit Card: (866) 532-9689
8. Citi, for your Macy's Credit Card: (866) 785-1079
9. Citi, for your retail and gas cards: (866) 683-0924

IF YOU CAN'T AFFORD TO MAKE THE MINIMUM PAYMENTS, HERE'S WHAT YOU SHOULD DO

The DOLP system works only if you can afford to make the minimum payments on all your cards. If you can't, please don't ignore the situation. That will only make things worse. Instead, reach out to the credit card companies. You'd be surprised how easy it can often be to work things out with them.

Here is what I suggest you do:

First, take advantage of Help With My Credit, a resource for struggling consumers created by a group of major card issuers, including Bank of America, Capital One, Citi, and Discover Card, plus the MasterCard and Visa networks. The service—which is available through both a toll-free number, (866) 941-1030, and a website (**www.helpwithmycredit.org**)—offers tips on managing your credit cards, communicating with the card companies, and finding an accredited credit counselor.

ASK THE CREDIT CARD COMPANIES ABOUT THEIR "DEBT-MANAGEMENT PLANS"

In an effort to prevent too many consumers from defaulting entirely on their debts, the credit card companies are now offering customers what they call debt-management plans. In a typical DMP, you can get your interest rate slashed (and sometimes eliminated entirely) in return for signing on to a guaranteed repayment program, in which payments are automatically debited from your checking account each month.

I've coached people who had their interest rates cut from 29% to zero as a result of signing up for a debt-management plan. On top of that, card companies are often willing to waive the monthly over-the-limit fees for DMP participants who've exceeded their credit limits.

The downside to these programs is that once you sign up, the credit card company will usually close your account or at least "freeze" it so you can't use it anymore. As we'll see in the next step, this can lower your credit score. Indeed, simply reporting that an account of yours has been placed on a payment or settlement plan can hurt your credit rating.

An explanation of how your credit record may be

affected and whether they will notify the credit bureaus is usually included in the contract the card companies make you sign before they let you begin a DMP. Before you sign, READ THE CONTRACT! It is crucial that you understand just what you're getting into (including what happens if you don't stick with the program).

Some credit card companies won't report your participation in a DMP if you ask them not to. Not paying your cards at all will hurt your score a lot more than being in a DMP plan. So will having your debt "charged off," which is what happens if you stop making payments altogether. Anyway, once your debt is paid down, your credit score will head back up again.

IF THE CREDIT CARD COMPANIES CAN'T HELP YOU, GET COUNSELING

The more work I do with credit-challenged people, the more I am becoming an advocate for consumer credit counseling. The only catch is that you have to find an honest company to work with. If you can—and it's not all that hard—the benefits can be enormous.

A good nonprofit credit-counseling agency will show you how to deal with your spending and create a payment plan to pay down your debt. They can also help you negotiate a debt-management plan with your creditors. In 2009, the credit card companies reached an agreement to make it easier for nonprofit credit-counseling organizations to help people in "hardship" situations. So ask about the new DMP rules when you call.

To get connected to a reputable nonprofit credit-counseling organization in your area, contact the National Foundation for Credit Counseling by calling toll-free (800) 388-2227 or by visiting their website at **www.debtadvice.org**.

In addition to the NFCC, you might also contact one of the following organizations for help with credit card debt:

Association of Independent Consumer Credit Counseling Agencies
www.aiccca.org
(866) 703-8787

Money Management International
www.moneymanagement.org
(866) 304-3818

Novadebt
www.novadebt.org
(866) 312-2887

Take Charge America
www.takechargeamerica.org
(877) 822-6060

AN IMPORTANT WARNING
ABOUT "NONPROFIT"
CREDIT COUNSELING

Not all credit counseling is created equal—and "nonprofit" doesn't necessarily mean fair or honest. You must investigate whomever you use before you use them. Check with the NFCC as well as the local office of the Better Business Bureau. In addition, ask the agency you're considering for references. You'll want to speak to at least five customers they have helped.

Do not use a credit-counseling service that does any of the following:
1. Charges you high up-front or monthly fees to enroll in a debt-management plan
2. Pressures you to make "donations" for their services
3. Tries to enroll you in a DMP without first really looking at your situation, reviewing your bills and budget, or educating you about basic money-management skills
4. Demands that you make payments to a DMP

BEFORE the credit card companies have accepted you into a program
5. Refuses to put in writing what they are promising to do to help you
6. Won't provide referrals of people they have helped

BEWARE OF "DEBT-SETTLEMENT" COMPANIES

As much as I am an advocate of credit counseling, I am leery of "debt-settlement" companies. These outfits offer to negotiate a settlement on your behalf with the credit card companies, often promising that they can "wipe out your debt or cut it in half." Their standard procedure is to tell you that if you stop paying the credit card companies and pay them instead, they will then be able to negotiate a settlement for you. In fact, there is no way to guarantee that your credit card company will accept a settlement from one of these companies.

Be very careful—it's amazing how many people I have seen ripped off by debt-settlement companies. One couple I did a "makeover show" with made payments to a debt-settlement outfit for a year—only to find they never paid off any of their credit card debt. It almost pushed them into bankruptcy.

TAKE ADVANTAGE OF THE
NEW CREDIT CARD ACT OF 2009
(IN EFFECT FEBRUARY 2010)

Now for some good news. As I mentioned earlier, as a result of new legislation enacted in 2009, the credit card industry has a new set of rules it must live by. Of course, you have to know your rights in order to be able to take advantage of them. So here is what you need to know about this new law.

It's called the Credit Card Accountability, Responsibility, and Disclosure Act of 2009 (or Credit CARD Act, for short). Although it was passed and signed into law in May 2009, it wasn't meant to take effect until February 2010. Under it, pretty much all the confusing and contradictory practices that were deliberately designed to get consumers to run up bigger balances are now prohibited. **Among other things, the act bans:**

1. Arbitrary "any time, any reason" rate increases on existing balances
2. Double-cycle billing (under which interest charges are based not on your current balance but on your average daily balance for the past two billing cycles—which means you could be charged interest on balances you paid off on time)
3. Universal default (a provision in credit card

agreements that gives the card company the right to jack up your interest rate if you are more than 30 days late paying any bill you owed to anyone— even a telephone or utility bill that has nothing to do with your credit card)
4. Late-fee traps such as weekend deadlines, due dates that change each month, and deadlines that fall in the middle of the day

At the same time, the new law requires banks to play fair with cardholders, which includes:

1. Applying partial payments to the highest interest balance first
2. Obtaining your permission before processing any transaction that would put you over your credit limit
3. Giving you a 45-day notice of any interest rate increases (which should be enough time to get yourself a new card with a better rate)
4. Giving you a reasonable amount of time to pay your monthly bills (at least 21 calendar days from time of mailing)
5. Writing credit card contracts and billing statements in clear, understandable English (including spelling out how long it will take you to pay off a balance if you make only minimum payments)

6. Clearly identifying temporary promotional rates as such—and keeping them in effect for at least six months

These new rules are great, but they won't enforce themselves. If you find a credit card company playing the old games with you, you need to get in the driver's seat and call them to account. Don't be shy about threatening to report them for violating the new law, if that's what you think they've done. As my grandmother used to tell me, you only get back what you ask for.

WHAT SHOULD I DO
IF MY CREDIT CARD DEBT HAS
ALREADY BEEN "CHARGED OFF"?

At some point, if you've gotten really behind on your credit card payments, the credit card company may throw up its hands and "charge off your debt"— meaning they write off the debt as a loss and sell it to a collection agency. If this has happened to you, here is what you need to do.

First, get copies of your credit reports (see page 68 for details on how to do this for free) and check if the debt shows up as having been "charged off." If it does, the damage is basically done. The charge-off will stay on your report for up to ten years, depending on the state, and it will bring down your credit score. But here's the good news: It also means that whoever is now calling you and harassing you to pay them is a collection agency that has bought your debt from the credit card company and is simply trying to make money on their investment.

TIME BARRED DEBTS— READ THIS BEFORE YOU SETTLE!

If you have fallen behind on payments on your debt, and you are now being harassed by a "debt collection agency" you may have rights you don't realize. The rules vary from state to state, but in most states there is a statute of limitations on your "time barred" debt—usually between three to ten years (in some cases longer). First, I want you to go to the government website, **www.ftc.gov**, and in the search box enter "time-barred debts." You may find that your debt has already cleared the date from which you can be sued by a creditor or debt collector. Also if you settle now, you may restart the time this negative mark appears on your credit record!

According to the FTC website most debts that have been delinquent more than seven years cannot appear on your credit report. Also there are laws to protect you from being harassed by creditors and debt collectors. Google Fair Debt Collection Practice (FDCPA) to know your rights.

Finally, if you think you are being unfairly harassed based on your rights, call the FTC toll-free hotline at 1-877-FTC-HELP. There is a wealth of information at **www.ftc.gov**. Do not settle anything, even if it's for pennies on the dollar, until you know your rights.

EXCELLENT—NOW LET'S LOOK AT YOUR CREDIT SCORE

You are taking action on your debt and doing great! Now it's time to consider your credit score. Let's go look at what you can do quickly not only to protect your score, but also to push it back up if it has dropped in the last year or two.

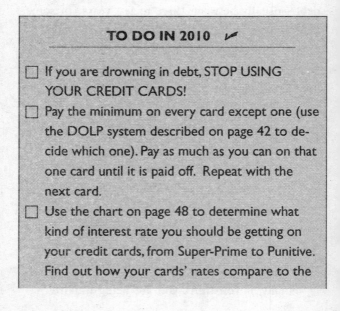

TO DO IN 2010 ✔

☐ If you are drowning in debt, STOP USING YOUR CREDIT CARDS!

☐ Pay the minimum on every card except one (use the DOLP system described on page 42 to decide which one). Pay as much as you can on that one card until it is paid off. Repeat with the next card.

☐ Use the chart on page 48 to determine what kind of interest rate you should be getting on your credit cards, from Super-Prime to Punitive. Find out how your cards' rates compare to the national averages. Armed with this knowledge, contact the credit card companies and ask for the lower interest rate you deserve.

☐ If you can't afford to make your minimum payments, ask your credit card companies about their debt-management plan—and if they can't (or won't) help you, get credit counseling from a reputable nonprofit agency recommended by the National Foundation for Credit Counseling.

☐ If your debt has been sold to a collection agency, prioritize this debt last and, when you are ready, negotiate to pay a fraction of the debt.

FIX AND PROTECT YOUR CREDIT SCORE

When was the last time you checked your credit score? More than likely, if you haven't checked it in the last 12 months, someone else has—maybe even your employer. Your credit score is your financial GPA. In good times, it determines how much interest you will pay on any kind of loan, from credit cards to your mortgage. Today, because of the credit crisis and the recession, having a high score is more crucial than it has ever been.

In the current environment, if you don't have a decent score, you may not be able to borrow money at all—even if you don't have other debt, and no matter how much interest you are willing or able to pay. In some cases, employers are refusing to hire people who have low scores. I recently gave a talk at the Pentagon and the military leaders there told me that they take credit scores so seriously that a bad one can actually prevent a soldier from being promoted. (That's because they consider someone with bad credit to be a security risk.)

This alone should tell you how important it is that you take your credit score seriously and work to get it back on track this year. What excites me (and should excite you) is that these days we know so much about what goes into calculating your credit score that aiming to raise your credit score by 50 to 100 points in less than a year—and often in less than six months—is a completely realistic goal.

YOUR GOAL THIS YEAR: A FICO SCORE OF 720— OR EVEN HIGHER

According to Fair Isaac Corp., the company that created the well-known FICO credit-scoring system, the median credit score in America today is 720 (meaning half of us score better than that and half of us score worse). In fact, Fair Isaac has been citing that same number since 2005, and most experts are skeptical of its accuracy. My guess is that the median

FICO score today is actually much lower than 720— probably somewhere in the mid-600s.

That said, I think 720 is a good number to aim for, and my goal for you is to get your FICO score up to that level this year—and ideally even higher. With this in mind, we're now going to look at exactly what you can do to make this a reality.

GET TO KNOW
YOUR CREDIT SCORE

Your credit score is not in fact a single number. Each of the three big national credit bureaus (Equifax, Experian, and TransUnion) has its own particular way of calculating our creditworthiness, as do literally hundreds of other lesser-known credit-reporting agencies.

Fair Isaac essentially invented the credit-scoring business back in 1989, and since then it's been considered the industry standard. All the big credit-reporting agencies base their individual scoring systems on mathematical models developed by Fair Isaac. This is probably why most people think the term "FICO score" is just another way of saying credit score (sort of the way people call all adhesive bandages Band-Aids and all facial tissues Kleenex and all photocopies Xeroxes).

According to Fair Isaac, more than 80% of lenders use FICO scores as part of their lending decision, so knowing your FICO score will give you a pretty darn good idea of whether or not you will be able to get a loan and how much it will probably cost you. What's more, while your FICO score may differ slightly from the scores calculated by the credit-rating agencies, it's not likely to be wildly different. In other words, if you have a great FICO score, chances are your other scores will be pretty good too. The opposite is also true: bad FICO score, bad credit bureau scores.

HOW DOES FICO DO IT?

Finding out your FICO score is simple enough. You just go to the FICO website (www.myfico.com). Figuring out how to improve your score isn't much harder. It's simply a matter of knowing the various factors that Fair Isaac uses to calculate it and seeing where you are weak. Where things get tricky is figuring out how to eliminate those weak spots.

On its website, Fair Isaac spells out how it weighs the various factors that go into calculating your score. They are, in order of importance:

1. **Payment History** (counts for 35% of your score)—Do you always pay your bills on time or do you have delinquencies? Are there any bankruptcies, liens, judgments, garnishments, et cetera, on your record? PAY ATTENTION TO

THIS! Simply paying your bills on time impacts more than a third of your score.

2. **Amounts Owed** (30%)—How much do you owe? What kinds of debt do you have? What proportion of your total credit limit is being used? (Most experts agree that a credit utilization of more than 50% will hurt your score. So if your Visa card has a credit limit of, say, $5,000, you want to avoid charging more than $2,500 on it at any one time.)

3. **Length of Credit History** (15%)—How long has it been since you opened your first credit account? How old is your oldest active account? (The average is 14 years; the longer your history, the better.) This is why you should no longer close old accounts you don't use—and why you should keep accounts open even after you have paid them off.

4. **New Credit** (10%)—How many accounts have you opened recently? How many recent inquiries by potential lenders? (Too much new activity is considered a bad sign.)

5. **Types of Credit Used** (10%)—How many different kinds of active credit accounts do you have? (A varied mix of credit—e.g., credit cards, installment loans, mortgages, retail accounts, etc.—is a plus; too much of one type is a minus.)

Basically, Fair Isaac takes the answers to all these questions and runs them through a complicated

series of calculations. The result is a number somewhere between 300 and 850. Anything over 700 is
considered good. Score 750 or higher and most
lenders will give you their best deals—even in today's
economy. On the other hand, a score below 620
means you will have to pay through the nose for
credit. And if you score less than 500, the likelihood
you can get a loan of any kind is very low.

What is amazing is how dramatically a difference
of just 50 to 100 points on your FICO score can
change everything when it comes to borrowing
money. The table below, similar to one you'll find on
the FICO website (**www.myfico.com**), shows how
differing FICO scores will affect the mortgage rates
banks are willing to offer you.

HOW FICO SCORES AFFECT YOUR MORTGAGE

Score	Interest Rate	Monthly Payment
760-850	4.85%	$1,584
700-759	5.08%	$1,624
680-699	5.25%	$1,657
660-679	5.47%	$1,697
640-659	5.90%	$1,779
620-639	6.44%	$1,885

Based on a $300,000, 30-year fixed-rate mortgage, as of 7/31/09

A 10-STEP ACTION PLAN
TO IMPROVE YOUR SCORE

So let's get started. The simple truth is that raising your score isn't that hard if you know what to do. It just takes time. As I noted above, it's mainly a matter of understanding the factors that FICO weighs and then figuring out which of them you can change for the better. Over the years, I've coached literally thousands of people on fixing their credit scores, and based on that experience I've developed a 10-step action plan to get your score up quickly and keep it there. I promise you—regardless of where you are starting from, if you follow this plan, in six months your score will be higher than you thought possible.

1. Get your credit report and check it for errors. There is only one place you can get a truly free copy of your credit report: **www.annualcreditreport.com**, a centralized service for consumers to request free annual credit reports run by the three nationwide consumer credit-reporting companies, Equifax, Experian, and TransUnion. You must do this first, because it's extremely likely that there are errors in your report. A 2004 survey by the National Association of State Public Interest Research Groups found that 79% of all credit reports contained incorrect information. There is no reason to believe that things have gotten any better since then. Once you get your report, go through it with a fine-tooth comb. If you find any damaging errors (for example, late payments that were actually paid on time or credit limits that are lower than they should be), get them corrected as quickly as possible. You can do this by sending the credit agency a certified letter that explains what information was inaccurate, including copies of documents (such as bank records or mortgage statements) that verify what you're saying, along with a copy of your credit report with the disputed information circled in red. Under the Fair Credit Reporting Act, both the credit-reporting agencies and the banks and merchants that provide them with data are required to correct inaccurate or incomplete information in your report when it's pointed out to them. (Occasionally, errors can help you, as when accounts you closed are listed as being open; don't feel obliged to correct these.) You can find sample correction letters on my website at **www.finishrich.com/ creditletters.**

2. Automate your bill paying so you never miss a deadline. Even if it's only a few days late, just one overdue payment—whether it's for your mortgage, a utility bill, an auto loan, a Visa account, or any of a hundred other credit obligations—can seriously damage your FICO score. FICO pays a lot of attention to whether you make a habit of missing due dates, so a series of late payments can really hurt your score. By the same token, a consistent record of on-time payments can improve it. Although FICO says it takes as much as **two years** of on-time payments to bump up your score, my experience is that if you pay all your bills on time for **a year,** your score will improve. This is why it is so important to set up the kind of automatic bill-payment plan I described in Step 3. If you haven't already done this, go back and reread that step and put the plan in place—it will protect your credit score and ultimately raise it.

3. Don't despair if you have missed payments. It's never too late to clean up your act. Get yourself current as quickly as you can and then stay current. Your score will begin to improve within **six months**— and the longer you keep it up, the more noticeable the increase will be. The negative weight FICO gives to bad behavior like delinquencies lessens over time, so as long as you stay on the straight and narrow, those black marks will eventually disappear from your record for good.

4. Keep your balance well below your credit limit. Of all the factors you can control—and improve quickly—how much you owe is probably the most powerful. What makes this especially important is that ever since the credit crunch first hit in the fall of 2008, credit card companies have been cutting customers' credit limits without warning—a practice that can be devastating to your credit score. Say you've got a $1,000 balance on card with a $2,000 credit limit—and then the card company slashes your limit to $1,000. Suddenly, you've gone from 50% credit utilization to being maxed out, and being maxed out can cost you as much as 100 points. This is why I recommend you use the DOLP plan I explained in Step 3 to pay down all your credit card balances as quickly as possible.

5. Spread your balances around—and don't borrow from Peter to pay Paul. Using one credit line to pay off another sets off FICO alarm bells—even if all you're doing is consolidating your accounts. All other things being equal, your FICO score will be higher if you have a bunch of small balances on a number of different cards rather than a big balance on just one or two.

6. If you rack up high balances, pay your credit card bill early. The "Amounts Owed" part of your FICO score is based on the balance due listed on your most recent credit card statements. So even if you pay your bills in full each month, running up high balances can still hurt your score. You can avoid this problem by paying down all or part of your bill *before* the end of your statement period, thus reducing the balance due that will be reported to FICO.

7. Hang on to your old accounts, even if you're not using them. Closing old accounts shortens your credit history and reduces your total credit—neither of which is good for your FICO score. If you have to close an account, close a relatively new one and keep the older ones open. Also, closing an account will not remove a bad payment record from your report. Closed accounts are listed right along with active ones.

8. Use your old cards. In the aftermath of the credit crunch, the credit card industry has begun closing inactive accounts. This can hurt your credit score, since it reduces the average age of your credit accounts. So my suggestion is that you pull out your old cards today and start putting at least one charge on each of them every month. This will keep the account open, which in turn will keep your credit history nice and long—and ultimately raise your score.

9. Demonstrate that you can be responsible. The best way to raise your score is to demonstrate that you can handle credit responsibly—which means not borrowing too much and paying back what you do borrow on time. Don't open new accounts just to increase your available credit or create a better variety of credit. This is especially true if you are just beginning to establish a credit history. Adding a lot of new accounts may look risky—and it will definitely lower the average age of your accounts, which can hurt your score if you don't have much of a track record. You should open new credit accounts only if and when you need them.

10. When you're shopping for a loan, do it quickly. When you apply for a loan, the lender will "run your credit"—that is, send an inquiry to one of the credit-rating agencies to find out how creditworthy you are. Too many such inquiries can hurt your FICO score, since that could indicate you're trying to borrow money from many different sources. Of course, you can generate a lot of inquiries doing something perfectly reasonable—like shopping for the best mortgage or auto loan by applying to a number of different lenders. The FICO scoring system is designed to allow for this by considering the length of time over which a series of inquiries are made. Try to do all your loan shopping within 30 days, so the inquiries get batched together and it's obvious to FICO that you are loan shopping.

BONUS TIP: Consider getting a credit score monitoring program. All of the three major credit bureaus, **www.equifax.com, www.experian.com,** and **www.transunion.com** offer an annual subscription service to monitor your credit record (most offer a free 30-day trial). The cost varies, depending on the offer—but this service can be invaluable to you to catch mistakes, and potentially any identity theft. Read the fine print before you sign up so you truly understand how much the service costs on a monthly basis and for how long they will bill you.

GOOD WORK!

You are on your way to a higher credit score and all the benefits that that provides: easier credit, lower interest rates on debt, and the trust of landlords, employers, and anyone inclined to check your trustworthiness. This lays the groundwork for the financial steps you have yet to take this year. So turn the page and let's get going.

TO DO IN 2010 ✔

☐ Go to www.annualcreditreport.com and get your free credit report.

☐ Consider signing up for an annual credit monitoring service at one of the major credit bureaus.

☐ Identify the factors that are keeping your score down (see pages 65–66). Take action on each one.

☐ Recheck your credit score in six months and again at the end of the year. Remember, your goal is 720 or higher.

REBUILD YOUR EMERGENCY SAVINGS

My Grandma Rose Bach used to tell me, "David, when the going gets tough, the tough have cash." In this, as in so many other things, she knew what she was talking about. Cash is king. Cash is security. Cash is protection. This is a lesson too many of us have learned the hard way in the recent downturn. It's one thing to have your credit cards maxed out and your home-equity line closed down by the bank. But then add in losing your job and your income—and, well, it can get pretty darn bleak.

The fact is that without a cash cushion, we are only one job loss or one emergency medical expense away from disaster. This is why we all need a rainy-day fund—a cushion of emergency money that can keep us afloat when times are tough. Unfortunately, in recent years, Americans have been really terrible about saving for a rainy day.

The good news is that there are signs millions of us have woken up to the need to increase our savings since the recession hit. After hovering around *zero* from 2005 through early 2008, the U.S. savings rate climbed past 5% in the spring of 2009. As the *Los Angeles Times* put it, "Given the economy's crash, many people clearly have gotten religion about saving money." And so should you—right now, this minute. Trust me, 2010 is the year to beef up your emergency money.

"WHERE DO I FIND THE MONEY?"

The biggest obstacle to setting up an emergency fund isn't convincing yourself that you should but convincing yourself that you can. I can't tell you how many students and clients of mine over the years have said to me something like this: "Come on, David, let's get real. I can barely make ends meet as it is. How can you possibly expect me to scrape together several thousand dollars and just leave it sitting in a bank account somewhere?"

My answer is that it's not as impossible as you think. To begin with, there's the Latte Factor: As I demonstrated in Step 2, you could easily be wasting 5 to 10 dollars a day—maybe a lot more—on unnecessary expenditures. This money would do you a lot more good in a rainy-day fund. Indeed, your first priority with any money you save by fixing your Latte Factor should be funding an emergency account.

Now, by themselves your Latte Factor savings may not be enough to build a big financial cushion very quickly. Especially if you're starting from zero, you're going to have to dig a bit deeper in order to get an emergency account fully funded anytime soon. This could mean temporarily giving up something that may be important to you but isn't actually essential—like premium cable or eating out or taking cabs instead of the bus. It may not be pleasant going without something you're used to, but, hey, this is a priority. And, anyway, the sacrifice won't go on forever. As soon as the balance in your rainy-day fund is where you need it to be, you can go back to watching HBO.

Again, I know what the objections to this approach are going to be. "But, David," people say to me, "even if I could reduce my spending on paper, I just don't have the willpower to actually do this in real life, day in and day out. It sounds like going on a diet—and we all know how those end up."

My answer to this is that there is a way to put aside money for your rainy-day account that doesn't involve willpower or discipline or stick-to-it-iveness.

What you do is make it automatic—that is, you arrange to have a portion of your pay automatically deducted from your paycheck and deposited in an account you've set up just for this purpose. (You could put your rainy-day money in the same account you use to pay your bills, but I don't think that's a good idea. When you keep your spending money and your emergency money in the same place, it's too easy to dip into the rainy-day fund for monthly expenses—and before you know it, your emergency fund will be gone.)

The great thing about automating your rainy day fund is that once you've set up your automatic saving system, you no longer have to think about it. And if you don't have to think about it, there's no chance you'll forget to do it—or, worse, change your mind and deliberately *not* do it.

THE FOUR RULES OF EMERGENCY MONEY

So how do you go about protecting yourself with a cushion of money? There are four basic rules.

1. **Set yourself a goal.** I've always said that every family should have a cash cushion of at least three months' worth of expenses. In other words, estimate how much you spend each month on essentials (mortgage or rent, utilities, food, health insurance,

etc.), multiply it by three, and that's your minimum goal for emergency savings. If you typically spend $3,000 a month, you want to have at least $9,000 put away in a reserve account not to be touched unless there's an emergency. Should you try to save more? Absolutely. How much more depends on what you feel you'll need to be able to "sleep well at night." I know people who keep *two years'* worth of expenses in a special account. Anything more than that is probably excessive, but better too much than too little.

2. Make it automatic. In Step 3 I said you have to make your emergency fund automatic. That means every single time your paycheck is deposited, your checking account is set up to automatically sweep money into a separate savings account you've set up for your rainy-day fund. I suggest you start by moving 5% of each paycheck to your emergency account until you reach the goal you set for yourself above.

3. Put it in the right place. Once you've made the commitment to funding a rainy-day account, the next decision you have to make is where to park it. I used to emphasize the importance of finding a place that would give you a reasonable return on your money. But these days, with interest rates at rock-bottom levels and the stability of many financial institutions still in question, I worry more about security. Of course, interest rates won't stay in the basement forever. But until they recover, which may not be for a long time, I'd focus less on the kind of return you're getting and more on making sure your emergency money is safe and accessible.

4. Leave it alone. The reason most people don't have any emergency money in the bank is that they have what they think is an emergency every month. What's a real emergency? It's *not* just having to buy a new dress for that special party. Or finding an amazing set of wheels for your car at a once-in-a-lifetime price. Or deciding you've got to get a new dishwasher because the old one is making noise. A real emergency is something that threatens your survival, not just your desire to be comfortable. So unless your family is about to go hungry or be thrown out into the street, you shouldn't be dipping into your emergency fund.

FIND YOUR "SLEEP WELL AT NIGHT" FACTOR

Here's a simple worksheet you can fill out right now to determine what amount of emergency savings you will need to sleep well at night.

Stop reading. Go and grab a pen or pencil and fill in the blanks on the next page to find out where you stand.

You don't need to pull out your checkbook to figure this out. Just estimate what you think you spend

---

"SLEEP WELL AT NIGHT" TEST

My monthly expenses currently total: $_____

I currently have $_____ saved in a money market or checking account.

This equals _____ [insert number] months' worth of expenses.

---

each month, what you know you have in the bank, and how many months' worth of expenses your current balance can cover.

Does the answer make you comfortable? If you're like most people, it probably doesn't. As I said before, most of us are literally living paycheck to paycheck. Actually, in most families, it's two paychecks to two paychecks. (Nearly three out of every four American homes are two-income households.) If one of those paychecks disappears, the family that depends on it can find itself upside down financially in a matter of weeks.

People used to find that hard to believe. But in the last year or two, how many heartbreaking stories have you seen on television or read in the newspaper about a family that went from a normal middle-class life to moving in with relatives in just a few months because Mom or Dad was laid off from work? I know I've seen too many. And what they all have in common is the fact that these newly homeless families didn't have any cash reserves to fall back on.

SO WHERE SHOULD YOU KEEP
YOUR RAINY DAY MONEY?

There is no point in setting up a rainy-day account if you can't be sure that the money will be there for you when you need it. A few years ago, this wasn't much of a concern. You could stick your emergency funds in a savings or money-market account at pretty much any reputable bank or brokerage and not worry about it. The only real question was whether or not your money was earning a reasonable amount of interest.

But the world has changed. Over the past few years, the U.S. financial system has taken a real beating. Some of the biggest financial-service companies came perilously close to collapsing—and a few actually did. So before you go rate-shopping for the best return you can earn on your rainy-day money, think about whether the bank or brokerage making you the best offer is an outfit you can really trust.

LOOK FOR THE FDIC SEAL
OF APPROVAL

There is one very easy way to know whether a bank can be trusted not to lose your money—check to see if it displays the official sign of the Federal Deposit Insurance Corporation.

The FDIC was originally created by the government during the Great Depression to restore confidence at a time when the nation's banking system seemed awfully shaky. As its name indicated, the FDIC's job was to insure deposits—and thus allow banks to tell nervous customers that even if the bank failed, their money (or at least a good chunk of it) would be safe.

The uncertainty hasn't been nearly that bad this time around, but by the fall of 2008 a new rash of bank failures had created so much nervousness that the FDIC decided to boost the amount of insurance it offers. So now, instead of providing just $100,000 worth of protection, FDIC insurance covers all deposit accounts at insured banks and savings associations—including checking, NOW, and savings accounts, money-market deposit accounts, and certificates of deposit (CDs)—up to a limit of $250,000 per individual per bank. (What the FDIC doesn't cover are deposits that have been invested in stocks, bonds, mutual funds, life insurance policies, annuities, or municipal securities, even if they were purchased from an insured bank.)

The increase is technically a temporary one, but it has been extended through the end of 2013. Similar action was taken by the National Credit Union Share Insurance Fund, which protects deposits at the nation's 7,800 federally insured credit unions.

Don't drive yourself crazy trying to figure out the rules. As the FDIC says on its website, "If you and your family have $250,000 or less in all of your deposit accounts at the same insured bank or savings association, you do not need to worry about your insurance coverage—your deposits are fully insured."

If you're lucky enough to have more than $250,000 in the bank, you can figure out how much protection you have by going online to the FDIC's "EDIE the Estimator" website at **www.fdic.gov/edie/**. EDIE, which stands for Electronic Deposit Insurance Estimator, can help you determine which of your bank accounts are covered by FDIC insurance and for how much.

FDIC coverage is as close to a sure thing as you can get in the financial world. You can check whether a particular bank or savings association has FDIC coverage by calling the FDIC toll-free at (877) 275-3342 or by going online to the FDIC's website (**www.fdic.gov**) and using its Bank Find tool. (From the home page, click the "Deposit Insurance" tab, then click the "Bank Find" link.)

PICKING YOUR BANK

As I write this in the summer of 2009, nobody—not regular banks, online institutions, credit unions, or brokerages—is paying more than 2% annual interest on a liquid account (whether savings or money market), and most are paying a lot less. At these low rates, on the modest amounts that you will be saving (maybe $15,000), the difference between a pretty good rate and a great rate may only amount to $100 or so a year. So while you shouldn't settle for a rock-bottom rate, you shouldn't stress too much about getting absolute top dollar. There are other, more important attributes to consider, such as:

1. Does the account require a minimum opening deposit? (On the day I checked, 9 of the 10 highest-interest money, market and savings accounts listed by **Bankrate.com** had opening minimums ranging from $100 to $5,000.)

2. Does it allow you to set up a systematic program that automatically transfers money from your regular checking account on a regular basis?

3. Does the account come with check-writing privileges, and if so, what's the smallest check you can write? Does it come with an ATM card? (Even though you're not going to use your checks or ATM card except in an emergency, it's nice to have them in case you ever need quick access to your funds.)

4. Does the bank charge a low-balance fee? (Some accounts charge you a fee of as much as $25 a month if your balance dips below a preset minimum.)

LET THE GOVERNMENT HELP YOU BUILD YOUR RAINY-DAY ACCOUNT

There is one other really safe and simple way to automatically create a rainy-day fund. If you are looking for a safe place to put your money, you can't do better than U.S. savings bonds, which are guaranteed by the full faith and credit of the United States government. What's more, the government's Treasury-Direct website (**www.treasurydirect.gov**) provides an incredibly easy way to invest as much or as little as you like in a variety of savings bonds and treasury securities through an automatic payroll deduction that you can basically set up online.

To be sure, savings bonds don't pay very much interest—if they pay any at all. As I write this in the summer of 2009, the government's inflation-indexed I Bonds are paying zero interest. Then again, the new Series EE Bonds (also known as Patriot Bonds) are paying a fixed annual rate of 0.70%, which is actually better than the average money market fund. For more information, visit the TreasuryDirect site and search for "individual savings."

FIX IT AND FORGET IT

Once you've made your rainy-day plan automatic, it will quietly add up. You can relax, breathe a little easier, and forget about it for a while. But keep an eye on the headlines for an upturn in interest rates. Eventually, the banks and the U.S. Treasury will start to pay competitive rates again. So check online and in the business section of your newspaper for the best rates possible. Use websites like **www.bankrate.com**, www.bankaholic.com, and www.bankingmyway.com where you can compare what's being offered and make sure your rainy-day fund is growing as fast as it can.

TO DO IN 2010 ✔

☐ Set a goal for your emergency fund that will let you sleep well at night—enough to cover a minimum of three months of basic expenses.

☐ In order to fund your emergency account, temporarily give up something you really like (like premium cable or eating out) but that isn't actually essential.

☐ Fund your emergency account automatically by having a portion of your pay direct-deposited from your paycheck or automatically transferred from your checking account into a separate account.

☐ Keep your emergency funds in an account that is FDIC-insured and accessible by check or ATM card—and then LEAVE IT ALONE!

RE-ENERGIZE YOUR RETIREMENT PLAN

Of all the terrible ways in which the recession affected people's lives, one of the most painful was what the Wall Street meltdown did to our retirement savings. Upward of 50 million Americans are putting aside money for retirement in one way or another, and with most people's 401(k) accounts and individual retirement arrangements heavily invested in stocks, virtually everyone took a major hit.

If you're contributing to a retirement account (and I do hope you still are), your nest egg probably lost close to a third of its value between the end of 2007 and the beginning of 2009—maybe more.

This has led a lot of people to throw in the towel. In a February 2009 survey by AARP, nearly 4 out of 10 workers said they had cut back the amount of money they were putting into their retirement accounts. Even worse, *one in five workers over the age of 45 said they had cut out their retirement contributions entirely.*

Giving up like this is one of the worst things anyone hoping to finish rich could do—and it's hard to think of a worse time than right now to be doing it. So if you are among those who have backed off from your retirement savings plan, or if you are thinking about changing course, then you need to hear this: **Given the economic surge that usually follows a deep recession, you couldn't pick a better time than today to recommit to a wealthy future by saving and investing for retirement.**

UPS AND DOWNS ARE NORMAL

The most important lesson to take from what's happened over the last few years is that the economy runs in cycles. Ups and downs may not be fun, but they are normal. Moreover, there are both good and bad things about both booms and busts.

When the market is up, our investments are worth more, but they also cost more. During the downturns, our investments are worth less, but they also cost less.

In other words, down markets present smart investors with a huge opportunity. Downturns are when you can buy stocks and other investments at bargain prices—that is, ON SALE. When the market goes back up—as it *always* has (and as I know it will again)—your investments will be worth much more than you paid for them.

As I write this in the summer of 2009, the market has already recovered a lot of the ground it lost in the meltdown. Between the beginning of March and the end of July in 2009, the Dow Jones Industrial Average jumped by roughly 2,250 points, from 6,626 to 9,176. That's a 38% increase in FIVE MONTHS. Will stock prices go straight back up to where they were in 2007? I doubt it, because Wall Street rarely moves like that. But while I don't know where the market will be when you read this, I do know this: You are either watching what is happening, wondering what is happening, or making something happen. Which is it?

You can't get rich watching and wondering. **You have to take action.**

YOU HAVE TO BE IN IT TO WIN IT

Most people I talk to were perfectly comfortable making investments with their retirement accounts *before* the market crashed. But having watched their retirement accounts lose as much as half their value, they are now extremely nervous about doing anything. Indeed, many people in their thirties and forties have given up completely. They are in what I call "do nothing" mode. A really good friend of mine named Chris says he will never invest in the stock market again. "The whole thing is rigged," he insists. "It's a fool's game, and I will never play the fool again."

Chris was so traumatized by watching his investments collapse that he's put all his retirement savings in a money-market account that pays less than 1% interest—and even though he's only 42, he insists that he's going to keep it there from now on. "I would rather live with a 1% return than run the risk of losing half my money in one year," he says.

Chris is a great guy and a smart guy—but he's dead wrong.

I totally understand the fear and anxiety the Wall Street and recession meltdown has generated. But there's such a thing as being too conservative. It may seem prudent, but there's a real problem with investing all your retirement savings in some super-safe asset paying a guaranteed rate of, say, 1% a year. *Your money is simply not going to grow fast enough.* Earning an annual return of 1%, it would take the rest of your lifetime (maybe longer) for you just to get back where you were before the meltdown.

YOU CAN MAKE UP YOUR LOSSES FASTER THAN YOU THINK

Earlier, I said that over the course of the stock market meltdown you probably saw your nest egg lose close to a third of its value. But that doesn't mean your

401(k) or IRA balance went down that much and stayed there. If you held on to your investments and kept contributing to your retirement account every month, you would have cut your losses considerably! In fact, according to the Employee Benefit Research Institute, 401(k) investors who stuck to their guns and kept putting money into their accounts throughout the meltdown actually saw their balances fall less than 9%.

YOU CAN CATCH UP

So don't think you're so far behind that you'll never be able to catch up. In fact, you can make up your losses much, much faster than you might think.

Let's say that during the Wall Street meltdown your 401(k) balance had dropped by 20%, from $100,000 down to $80,000. If you kept contributing $500 a month, do you know how long it would take you to get back to where you were before the crash?

Would you guess three years? Five years? Ten years?

How about less than two?

Even though the recession has taken its toll, more than 70% of companies with 401(k) plans still match all or part of their employees' 401(k) contributions. The most common match is 50 cents for every dollar you put in up to a total of 6% of your annual pay. According to calculations made by the Employee Benefit Research Institute for CNNMoney.com, if your employer kicked in an additional "match" of $250 a month and your investments earned just 4% a year, you'd be back even within about 18 months.

This is truly your Start Over deal!

Remember Step 1 in this book? It said that you must recommit to believing in the possibility of living and finishing rich. Your first step toward fixing your retirement plan in 2010 is to recommit to keeping up with your retirement contributions and reclaiming your faith in your future financial freedom.

WHERE IS YOUR MONEY RIGHT NOW?

Before you can decide if you need to make any changes in how your retirement money is invested, you need to know where your money currently is and how you really did in the downturn. So here's a question to ask yourself:

Do you know what you are invested in RIGHT NOW?

Every day, people tell me their retirement accounts "stink," but when I ask them what their investments are, they have no clue.

"David," they say, "it's in my 401(k) plan."

Great, what company manages it?

"Oh, I don't know—I think it's a Fidelity 401(k). Are they any good?"

Actually, Fidelity is great and they offer many options for you to invest in. What funds do you own?

"No idea. All I know is that my money is in a Fidelity account and it went down 50%."

You may think I'm exaggerating, but I have conversations exactly like this every single day. The point is that you have to know what you own! When it comes to your retirement savings, ignorance will kill you. **So pull out your statement today—right now!—and FIND OUT what your retirement savings are invested in.** It's your money, and you need to know this—no excuses.

HOW DID YOU REALLY DO?

What did you discover? If the stock market as a whole is down 20% and your retirement account is down 10%, you're not doing that badly. I know it feels terrible to have lost so much. But in fact, you did better than the market as a whole. Keep in mind that while stocks may have fallen by 40% between October 2007 and October 2008, most retirement accounts didn't actually lose that much because they were not 100% invested in stocks. They were invested in a combination of stocks, bonds, and cash.

So despite whatever hits you may have taken during the meltdown, you may have actually gotten through it pretty well—or at least okay, even though it doesn't feel like it. How can you know if this is the case? It's easy. Pull out your statements and review how your investments did compared to others like them. Every mutual fund is part of a class—it might be large-cap stocks or intermediate-term bonds—and is identified as such in the informational materials the fund company sends you. You can compare a particular fund's performance to that of its class as a whole at a website like **www.morningstar.com**. Or, even easier, you can ask your 401(k) provider or mutual-fund company for a report that compares your funds against the indexes they are supposed to be matching or beating.

Whichever route you prefer, do it today!

HOW MUCH RISK IS RIGHT FOR YOU?

The second question you need to ask about your retirement investments is how risky they are, and whether it is a level of risk that is appropriate for your age and temperament. Basically, the idea is that when you are young you should be willing to be aggressive and take risks in order to achieve high returns. But as you get older and your retirement date approaches, your investment priorities should shift from growth to what's called capital preservation (that is, not losing what you've managed to accumulate). As a result, what's called the asset allocation (the variety of types of investments) in your portfolio should gradually become more conservative, moving away from volatile investments like stocks and toward more stable ones like bonds and cash.

There's an old rule of thumb that says the percentage of your portfolio invested in fixed-income securities (e.g., bonds and bond funds) should equal your age, with the rest being invested in equities (stocks and stock funds). So if you're 25 years old, 25% of your retirement savings should be in fixed income and 75% in equities. And if you're 55, 55% should be in fixed income and 45% in equities.

THE ADVANTAGES
OF TARGET-DATE MUTUAL FUNDS

Of course, if you are going to link your asset allocation to your age, you are going to have to rebalance your portfolio every year, making sure you have more of your retirement assets in bonds and less in stocks as you get older. You may also have to rebalance your investments if either the stock market or the bond market undergoes a sudden shift. For example, if the stock market soars, so will the value of your equity investments. And unless you sell off a bunch of stocks, that will unbalance your carefully allocated portfolio. Rebalancing forces you to "sell high and buy low," the first principle of smart investing.

Keeping on top of all this can be a pain. But there is an easy way to get around the need to rebalance every year (if not more often). You can use what are called target-date funds. These funds are specifically designed for retirement savings. They get their name from the fact that each is labeled with a particular target date (2015, 2020, 2025, etc.), indicating it's meant for a person who plans to retire in or near that year. You pick the right year for you, and the fund automatically ensures that you will have the appropriate asset allocation (that is, the right mix of investments in stocks, bonds, and cash) for someone your age—more aggressive when you're younger, gradually becoming more conservative as you approach retirement.

Because of their automatic nature, target-date funds have become enormously popular, especially among younger savers. More than 80% of all 401(k) plans offer them as an option, and as of the middle of 2009, they held an estimated $187 billion in assets. That still amounted to only about 7% of all 401(k) assets, but target-date funds are growing so fast that some experts believe that by 2015 they will account for a third of all savings in 401(k)s and other defined-contribution plans.

Every major fund family now offers these funds, and they are probably part of your 401(k) plan. But they are not all alike. While all of them subscribe to the basic idea that as you approach retirement age you should be moving away from stocks and toward fixed-income securities, they differ widely on what that balance should be. Some funds aim to be 90%

invested in bonds and cash by the target date; others keep you heavily in stocks right up to the end.

With such wide variations, it's critically important that you look closely at the particulars of any target-date fund you might be offered—specifically, how it adjusts the balance between stocks, bonds, and cash as the target date approaches. My suggestion is that you err on the side of safety. A simple way to do this is to buy a fund with a target date earlier than your actual retirement date. So if you are planning to retire in 2020, go with a 2015 fund—that way your savings will be invested a bit more conservatively than if you had bought the "correct" year's fund.

GETTING HELP

Are you still feeling uncertain about your choices? If so, I strongly recommend you get help from a financial professional.

As part of their 401(k) programs, many employers have arrangements with professional retirement-planning advisory firms that will custom-build and manage a retirement portfolio for you, often for a very low price. One of the leading examples is Palo Alto–based Financial Engines (**www.financialengines.com**), which was founded by Nobel Prize–winning economist William Sharpe in 1996 and now manages retirement plans for employees of more than 750 major companies as well as customers of virtually every big 401(k) provider. See if your company offers Financial Engines or a similar firm as a service. They usually charge an annual fee that ranges between 0.15% and 0.35% of the assets they are managing for you.

In addition, the fund companies themselves generally offer their own advisory services. For instance, Fidelity, Charles Schwab, and Vanguard offer online services you can use to create an asset-allocation plan for yourself. They will also provide some hand-holding advice on which funds to use. So check with your 401(k) fund provider to see what it can do for you. Don't put this off—make that call now!

GETTING HELP IF YOU'RE NOT IN A 401(K) PLAN

If you are not in a 401(k) plan but rather are saving for retirement with an IRA and you want guidance, then you may want to get low-cost advice on your own. This may sound complicated and expensive, but it doesn't have to be.

For "do-it-yourself investors," I recommend that you consider working with a discount broker like E*Trade or TD Ameritrade. Both of these firms offer tremendous services to help you build a portfolio of exchange-traded mutual funds (known as ETFs, for short). I generally prefer to invest in ETFs rather than professionally managed mutual funds. The costs of

ETFs are much lower, and over the long term I believe you will make more money.

E*Trade
www.etrade.com
(800) ETRADE-1; (800) 387-2331

E*Trade offers a program called Online Advisor that will recommend an asset-allocation structure for you, compare it with your current holdings, and then suggest investments that will get you where you need to be. It requires a $10,000 minimum investment to start, and the fees run between 0.5% and 0.75% of the size of your account. So if you're investing $10,000, you can get it done for $75 a year. (There are also trading commissions to pay on top of that, but once you get your portfolio built, you're not likely to be doing much trading, so that cost will be small too.)

TD Ameritrade
www.tdameritrade.com
(800) 454-9272

TD Ameritrade offers a similar service called Portfolio Guidance. You can find it by clicking the "Planning & Retirement" tab on their home page. The specific plan you want is called Self-Directed Amerinvest. It will build you a portfolio with low-cost ETFs and rebalance it for you automatically. Fees start at 0.75% for the first $100,000 of assets, and you need to invest at least $25,000 to start.

In addition, you might want to consider these firms:

Fidelity Investments
www.fidelity.com
(800) FIDELITY; (800) 343-3548
Fidelity offers a Portfolio Advisory Service that will build you a portfolio appropriate for your age and risk tolerance. Annual fees range from 0.25% to 1.1% of your assets, and a minimum investment of $50,000 is required.

Charles Schwab
www.schwab.com
(866) 855-9102
In Schwab's Managed Portfolios program, portfolio managers will make all investing decisions for you, including mutual-fund research and selection, with the aim of creating a diversified mutual-fund portfolio matched to your financial goals and risk tolerance. The minimum investment required is $25,000 for an IRA, $50,000 for all other accounts. The annual fee, which includes all trades placed by Schwab, is 0.50% for up to $250,000.

Vanguard
www.vanguard.com
(877) 662-7447
Vanguard offers a service where you work with a cer-

tified financial planner to create a customized plan based on your long-term goals. After a personal consultation, you'll receive asset-allocation and fund recommendations, along with a savings analysis to see if you're on the right track. Their service requires a minimum investment of $100,000 and their fees start at $250 per year. Vanguard has an asset-allocation fund, the Star Fund (VGSTX), that is professionally managed by Vanguard and does all the asset-allocation rebalancing for you (and you only need $1,000 to start investing in an IRA). This is my favorite no-load, low-cost asset-allocation fund.

A NEW SERVICE
WORTH CHECKING OUT

MarketRiders
www.marketriders.com
(866) 990-ETFS

MarketRiders is a new company, so its track record is limited, but I think these guys are onto something smart. The idea is "do-it-yourself investing." For a nominal fee of $9.95 a month, their website will design a portfolio of ETFs based on your circumstances and tolerance for risk. You can then buy the funds through a discount broker like E*Trade or TD Ameritrade. Once you've made the investments, MarketRiders will track your portfolio and alert you via email when they think you need to rebalance your account.

NOW MAX IT OUT

Now that you're feeling confident about your investment choices, here is the number-one thing you can do to ensure a richer retirement: Max out your plan. In other words, commit yourself to making the maximum contribution your company's plan allows.

The truth is, most of us haven't socked away nearly enough in retirement savings. According to the Center for Retirement Research at Boston College, the typical worker had assets worth a total of just $56,000 in his retirement accounts at the end of 2008. The Employee Benefit Research Institute's 2009 Retirement Confidence Survey painted an even bleaker picture. It found that 40% of all workers have less than $10,000 in savings.

In other words, most people have socked away barely enough to get them through a single year of retirement—and many don't even have that much. So unless you're planning to work until you drop, what you need to be doing now is putting away more.

HOW TO SAVE $750 A MONTH— AT A COST OF ONLY $350

I can hear your protests now: "But, David, I can't afford to put away more than I do." Here's why I know that you *can*. If you are investing using a retirement plan like a 401(k) or an IRA, then every dollar you invest actually costs you less than 70 cents.

How is that possible? It's the magic of pretax investing. As we know all too well, every time we earn a dollar, before that dollar ever makes it onto our paycheck, the government grabs something like 27 cents in federal income withholding taxes (often more—and before very long probably a *lot* more). On top of that, local governments may grab another five cents in city and state withholding. (Exactly how much depends on where you live.) And then there are Social Security taxes, Medicaid, and unemployment.

But it doesn't have to be that way. If you are contributing to a pretax retirement account—like a 401(k) plan or an IRA—the money you put in is entirely TAX-DEDUCTIBLE (up to certain limits). In other words, it comes in off the top, before Uncle Sam takes his bite. You get to keep the whole dollar for you and your future.

What this means is that if you decided to start saving an extra $50 per paycheck in your 401(k) or IRA, you would *not* see your take-home pay go down by $50. In fact, it would go down only by $35. The $15 that normally would have gone to the taxman goes to your future instead.

And if your employer has a matching program, you may be able to add another $25 to that $50. In other words, a $75 investment is costing you only 35 bucks. If you have ever shopped a sale, how can you refuse a bargain like this? The bottom line is that you can save much more than you think, easier than you think.

What I'm talking about here, of course, is the tried-and-true concept known as "paying yourself first"—putting some of your hard-earned wages into your retirement account *before* the taxman takes his cut. I'm going to be blunt here. If you want to be financially secure and ultimately finish rich, you have to do this. There is absolutely no way to start over and finish rich if you allow the government to continue muscling in ahead of you. I mean, think about it—how can you possibly expect to get anywhere if you're willing to give up 30 to 40 cents out of every dollar you make *before you ever have a chance to spend—or invest—a penny of it?*

There's no getting around it. You must PAY YOURSELF FIRST. Not doing it is simply not an option.

IF YOU ARE NOT IN THE GAME, GET IN THE GAME

By now, I hope you are convinced that there has never been a better time to be saving for your future. Even if you have to start small.

So if your employer offers a 401(k) plan and you are not already enrolled, call your benefits office today and find out how to sign up. If your company doesn't have a 401(k) plan, you will need to set up your own individual retirement arrangement (IRA). Details on how to do this—and everything else you need to know about IRAs for 2010 and beyond—are available in a special report I've posted on my website. You can download it for FREE from **www. finishrich.com/retirementreport**.

DEPEND ON
YOUR YOUNGER SELF NOW

No one is going to take care of you or me the way we would like to live when it comes time to retire. There are simply not enough taxable dollars to go around to support the 150 million Americans who will reach retirement age over the next 50 years.

You know it and I know it. All we can count on is ourselves.

There's only one real way to guarantee yourself a comfortable and secure retirement: You need to DEPEND ON YOUR YOUNGER SELF NOW. You will save yourself tomorrow by deciding to save yourself today.

The time to take action is now. So please take action. Get back in the game. Increase the amount you are saving for retirement. Decide to pay yourself first. Review what you are invested in and fix it if it needs fixing—and get help if your plan offers professional guidance. This is the heart of your "Start Over" plan. Please get it going today. I promise you—your older self will thank you later.

TO DO IN 2010 ✔

☐ If you have stopped contributing to your retirement account, start again immediately.

☐ If your employer offers a 401(k) or similar retirement plan, make sure you're signed up and contributing. If you don't have a 401(k) at work, you should have your own IRA.

☐ Know exactly where your money is invested. Pull out your retirement account statement and find out what your savings are invested in.

☐ Using www.morningstar.com, compare your investments' performance to others in the same asset class.

☐ Determine what level of risk you're comfortable with—and what's right for someone your age. Then make sure your investments reflect that.

☐ Consider "target date" mutual funds so you don't have to rebalance your investments yourself every year.

☐ If you don't feel comfortable making these decisions yourself, get help from a qualified financial professional. Ask your employer if your plan offers a free or fee-based advisory service, or find one from the several recommended in this chapter.

☐ Increase your retirement contributions today, and if you don't feel the pinch, raise them some more. Your goal is to reach the maximum contribution allowed.

MAKE IT AUTOMATIC

If there is one thing you must do in 2010 in order for your "Start Over" plan to work, it is this: *YOU MUST MAKE YOUR PLAN AUTOMATIC.*

In the steps in this book so far, you've learned the few simple things you must do this year to get your finances back on track. Most of them involve taking chunks of what you earn and putting them aside for particular purposes—funding an emergency account, contributing to a retirement plan, paying down credit card debt, and so on. These are all tried-and-true strategies, and taken together, they will enable you to start over and finish rich.

However, the single most important thing I've learned from working with hundreds of clients as a financial advisor, and now from coaching through my books and seminars, is that the only plans that work are the ones that are automatic! Discipline simply doesn't work. Working harder to save money simply doesn't work. Discipline and hard work take time, and if your plan requires hundreds of separate actions, month after month, year after year, it will fall by the wayside when the going gets tough. Sure, we'd all like to be prudent and disciplined and thrifty. But how many of us actually are? Over the years, I've had countless clients who insisted they were disciplined enough to do it themselves. In fact, there was only one who was actually able to stick to a financial plan manually (that is, by sitting down and writing himself checks every month) for any length of time.

The government knows we can't be trusted. That's why it came up with withholding tax. It knows that the only way to guarantee that you will pay your tax bill is to take the money from your paycheck AUTOMATICALLY before you can spend it.

This is a strategy worth imitating. You need to do for yourself what the government did for itself: Set up a system that guarantees you won't have spent all your money on other things before you get around to putting your hard-earned dollars where they are supposed to go—to ensuring a richer future. Set it up so that you only have to take action *once* and you guarantee your success.

Even if you think you're the most disciplined person in the world, don't regard the automatic part as an optional extra. There is a reason it has its own step in this book. If you are serious about getting back on track, it's not enough to say you're going to do it. You've also got to make the process automatic.

If you follow the action steps in this chapter—along with the diagram on page 116—you will truly have a foolproof, no-brainer, "set it and forget it" financial plan that, I promise you, will work. The plan is based on the one I laid out in my book *The Automatic Millionaire,* but I've updated it for 2010. It will take you less than an hour to get it organized. Read the steps and follow the diagram. It's easy and, YES, YOU REALLY CAN DO IT.

Are you ready?

Then let's go make it automatic!

MAKING IT AUTOMATIC IN LESS THAN AN HOUR

1. **Pay yourself first automatically.** In Step 6, I explained the critical importance of paying yourself first—having at least 5% of what you earn deducted from your paycheck and deposited directly into a 401(k), IRA, or similar qualified retirement account *before* the government takes its bite of withholding tax. Ideally, this deduction should total 12.5% of your income (the equivalent of one hour's worth of work each day). But whatever you can manage, you must

make the process automatic. The good news is that payroll deduction is a standard feature of most 401(k) plans, so as long as you're signed up, your contributions will be automatically deducted from your paycheck. If you had made your 401(k) automatic, you would have been perfectly set up to benefit from the stock market crash of 2008. While other people were panicking and pulling their money out of the market (selling low), you would have been investing all the while, buying when stocks were at their cheapest.

If you're not eligible for a 401(k) or similar plan and as a result use an IRA for your retirement savings, you'll have to create your own automatic "pay yourself first" program. Tell the bank or brokerage where you have your IRA that you want to set up a *systematic investment plan.* This is a plan under which money is automatically transferred on a regular basis into your IRA from some other source (such as a payroll deduction). Most banks and brokerage firms will handle all the arrangements for you, contacting your employer's payroll department on your behalf and dealing with all the paperwork. (If your employer doesn't offer payroll deduction, you can have your retirement-plan contribution automatically moved from your checking account to your IRA—ideally, the day after your paycheck clears. Most banks have free online bill-paying services that allow you to schedule regular automatic payments of specified amounts to anyone you want.)

2. Deposit your paycheck automatically. If your employer uses a computerized payroll system, you should be able to arrange with your company's personnel or human resources department to have your pay automatically wired directly into your bank account. This is known as direct deposit. It gets your pay into your account without delay—and saves you the trouble of wasting a lunch hour every week or two waiting in line at the bank with a paper check.

3. Fund your emergency account automatically. In Step 5, I explained the importance of maintaining an emergency cash cushion of at least three months' worth of expenses in an FDIC-insured bank account (*not* your regular checking account but a separate one set up specially for this purpose). Until this emergency account is fully funded, you should have at least 5% of your paycheck directly deposited into it. Again, if your employer doesn't offer payroll deduction, arrange to have your bank automatically transfer the money from your checking account the day after your paycheck clears.

4. Fund your dream account automatically. What's a dream account? This is where you save the money that is going to pay for your home, car, wedding, trip to Hawaii, new boat, guitar, ski lessons, cooking school—whatever your dream happens to be. Most dreams require CASH, and because most people don't have the cash, they either borrow to pay for their dream (whether by putting it on their credit cards or taking out an actual loan), or they never make the dream a reality. In some ways, your dream account is the most important account you will have, because living your dreams is where the excitement of life really is. As with your emergency fund, use either payroll deduction or your bank's online bill-pay service to have a percentage of your paycheck automatically transferred into an FDIC-insured account set up just for this purpose. If your dream is at least three years away from fulfillment, start investing the money more aggressively once your dream savings total $10,000.

5. Pay your credit card bills automatically. Call all your credit card companies and arrange to have all your bills come due on the same day of the month—ideally, 10 days after your paycheck is normally deposited. (Virtually every credit card company will work with you to change your due date if you ask them.) Then use your bank's online bill-paying service to automatically make the minimum payment for each of your cards five days before the bill is due. (If your bank doesn't offer free online bill paying, think about switching to one that does.) If you want to pay more than the minimum on any of your cards—and if you follow the plan I lay out in Step 3, you will—you can write a check for the extra amount. Making your minimum payments automatic ensures that you will never miss a payment deadline and get hit with late fees or penalty interest rates.

6. **Pay all your monthly bills automatically.** There are two kinds of monthly bills: regular ones that are always the same amount (like mortgage, rent, or car payments) and those where the balance due sometimes varies (like phone bills or cable and Internet charges). You can automate payment of the unchanging bills by using your bank's online bill-paying service to have them automatically debited from your checking account each month. And you can automate payment of the variable ones by arranging to have them charged to one of your credit cards. As long as you keep your checking account adequately funded and you have sufficient credit available on your card accounts, this will protect you from ever missing a payment due date. My entire financial life is automated this way. As a result, all my bills are always paid on time, whether I am in town or not, and I never get hit with late fees or penalties.

7. **Give to charity automatically.** As I explain in the bonus chapter that starts on page 181, giving back is an integral part of starting over. But instead of making a lump-sum contribution once a year (which you might or might not actually get around to), arrange to automatically fund the charity of your choice through a series of small regular contributions—say, somewhere between 1% and 10% of each paycheck. Most charities will happily agree to charge your credit card or accept an automatic debit from your bank account. Choose a charity that you care about

and become a monthly giver. The charity will be thrilled, and you will feel good doing it.

You've now made your financial life automatic. Congratulations! If you do nothing else from this point forward, you have set yourself up for success.

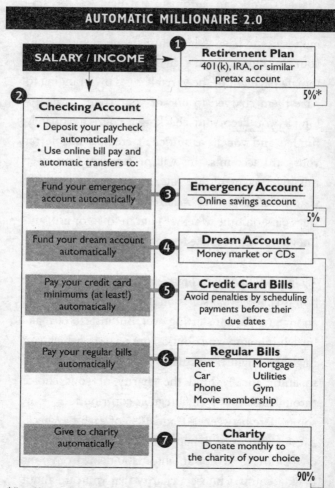

AUTOMATIC MILLIONAIRE 2.0

SALARY / INCOME

1 Retirement Plan
401(k), IRA, or similar pretax account
5%*

2 Checking Account
• Deposit your paycheck automatically
• Use online bill pay and automatic transfers to:

Fund your emergency account automatically → **3 Emergency Account**
Online savings account
5%

Fund your dream account automatically → **4 Dream Account**
Money market or CDs

Pay your credit card minimums (at least!) automatically → **5 Credit Card Bills**
Avoid penalties by scheduling payments before their due dates

Pay your regular bills automatically → **6 Regular Bills**
Rent   Mortgage
Car   Utilities
Phone   Gym
Movie membership

Give to charity automatically → **7 Charity**
Donate monthly to the charity of your choice
90%

* Your ultimate goal should be to save at least 12.5% for retirement, one hour of your daily income.

REBUILD WITH REAL ESTATE

Are you shocked to read the title of this chapter? Don't be. For all that we've been through with the mortgage meltdown and the collapse of housing prices in recent years, the power of real estate hasn't changed. The fact is, if you are serious about finishing rich, you will eventually need to own some property. And whether you are currently a renter or owner, there may never be a better time to put your real estate plan in place than right now.

YES, YOU CAN STILL GET RICH IN REAL ESTATE

This is truly an unprecedented time to get into real

estate. As I write this, a record number of homes are for sale and prices in many markets are down anywhere from 25% to 50%. In short, it's the most amazing buyer's market we've seen in decades. **There are deals everywhere—and, as a result, homeownership is more affordable than it has been in years.** Indeed, in April 2009, the homeowner affordability index hit 179—meaning that a typical American family was earning 179% of the income necessary to qualify for a mortgage on a typical home—its second-highest level on record.

The opportunity to be a buyer in a market like this comes along maybe once every 20 years, so this is not a time to be sitting on the sidelines. The fact is, the fundamentals of real estate have not changed. Real estate has always had booms and busts—but over the long term, real estate makes people rich. Certainly, many people have lost fortunes in real estate over the last few years. But many others are now making fortunes. They are taking advantage of the current unprecedented real estate market to build wealth by refinancing their current mortgages, buying bigger homes or investment properties, or even getting into the housing market for the first time.

The question for you is: What is your real estate plan? You must have one. To put it plainly, real estate is still the best route to riches there is.

So let's get going.

HOMEOWNERSHIP REMAINS ONE OF THE BEST—IF NOT *THE* BEST— INVESTMENTS YOU CAN MAKE

To begin with, it's important to remember that the real estate news is not all bad. There are currently 75 million homeowners in America, and not all of them are in trouble. In fact, what isn't reported every day is that more than 90% of homeowners are NOT behind on their mortgage payments or in jeopardy of losing their homes. Furthermore, the average American who owns a home is not just a little richer than the average renter. He or she is a *lot* richer.

According to the most recent Federal Reserve's Survey of Consumer Finances, the net worth of a typical homeowner is 46 times higher than that of a typical renter. Over the long haul, homeownership remains one of the best—if not *the* best—investments you can make. In fact, in the 12 years from 1997 to 2009, U.S. homeowners have seen the values of their properties appreciate by an average of 5.4% a year.

THE DARK CLOUDS OF REAL ESTATE ARE CLEARING—IT'S TIME TO ACT!

These numbers may not be much consolation if you bought your house at the top of the market in 2006. But the fact is that the tide is turning. As I write this in

August 2009, Standard & Poor's has just reported that after free-falling for three years, the rapid decline in home prices has finally begun to slow, while new construction and sales of previously owned homes are climbing faster than anyone had expected.

None of this means a quick recovery is necessarily in the cards. But the statistics do show a "bottoming" of the real estate market—meaning things are not likely to get any worse, and will probably start getting better from here on out. By the time you read this, the real estate market will almost certainly be looking even better. So the waiting period is over—it is time for you to act.

WHAT KIND OF REAL ESTATE PERSON ARE YOU?

When it comes to real estate, there are three kinds of people: those who own, those who want to own, and those who own and want to own more.

What you should do next depends on which one of these categories you fit into. So let's look at each of them and see what your course of action should be.

I'M AN OWNER AND MY HOME IS DOWN IN VALUE—WHAT DO I DO?

If you're already a homeowner, chances are your house isn't worth what it used to be. So what do you do? Well, for starters, you need to ask yourself what it is you *want* to do. If your answer is "I like my home and I want to keep it"—then there are two more questions you need to consider: Can you afford to keep your home, and do you have the best financing for your situation?

In no case should you be spending more than 35% of your gross income on housing costs. These include your mortgage payment, taxes, homeowner's association or condo fees (if any), insurance, and taxes. And truthfully, 35% of your gross income is an awfully big chunk of your money. It would be better to keep the amount you spend on housing down around 25% of your gross income.

IT'S TIME TO REFINANCE TO A SAFE SMART MORTGAGE

Just because you can afford to make your mortgage payments doesn't mean you have the right kind of financing. I have always recommended (and been criticized for recommending) that homebuyers stick with a "plain vanilla" mortgage—that is, a 15-year or 30-year fixed mortgage. The advantage to a simple mortgage like a 15- or 30-year fixed is that (1) you know exactly what your payments are going to be for the life of the mortgage; and (2) you pay down principal with every payment, thus reducing the amount you owe and building equity every month.

While the total cost of a 15-year fixed mortgage is

a lot less, I personally have always urged homebuyers to go with a 30-year mortgage—and make extra payments. The fact is, you can always pay off a 30-year mortgage in 15 years by paying more than you have to each month. (Your bank can help you calculate exactly how much extra to add.) But if you or your spouse loses a job or your finances get tough, you'll appreciate the lower monthly payment a 30-year mortgage requires.

So my recommendation is that if you plan to be in your home more than another five years and you have anything but a 15- or 30-year fixed mortgage— say, one of those adjustable-rate deals that have gotten so many people in trouble—then you should refinance NOW. Rates are at historic lows as I write this—but it won't last forever.

The best place to start mortgage shopping is online. First, go to a website like **www.lendingtree.com** or **www.bankrate.com** and see what mortgage lenders are offering. Then call your current lender and ask if he can match the best deal you found online.

WHAT YOU NEED TO KNOW
ABOUT REFINANCING

Most banks are happy to do refinancing deals. In fact, the bulk of the mortgage banking business in 2009 was in refinancing. So don't be shy about asking your bank for a "refi."

When you compare mortgages, you will need to make note of the annual percentage rate (APR), whether the lender is charging you "points" up front (you don't want this), and what the closing costs will be (including fees for appraisals, title search, title insurance, credit reports, etc.).

Refinancing makes sense only if the savings you enjoy from lower interest payments more than cover the cost of closing the new mortgage. If you are going to be in your home for more than another three years, you'll generally come out ahead as long as your new interest rate is at least one full percentage point lower than what you are currently paying. Have your bank run a "break-even analysis" for you. They can do this in a matter of minutes and tell you, "Yes, the cost of refinancing will be paid off in 28 months [or whatever]." You need to know this before you pull the trigger on the refinance.

DON'T WALK AWAY JUST BECAUSE YOUR HOME IS "UNDER WATER"

One of the most common complaints I hear from people is that because their home is "under water" (meaning it is worth less than they owe on their mortgage), the bank won't let them refinance. At this point, many people decide it is no longer worth their while to even try to keep their homes. Indeed, a recent study by the University of Chicago's Booth

School of Business and Northwestern University's Kellogg School of Management showed that one out of every four home-mortgage defaults in 2008 and 2009 was the result of a calculated decision to walk away from a paper loss. It had nothing to do with being able to afford the mortgage.

Walking away from your house in this way can be a huge mistake. Take Adam, a guy I recently met who owned a beachfront house in Florida. Adam told me he had paid $820,000 for it in 2007 and was carrying a $650,000 mortgage. Problem was, it was now worth less than $600,000. So even though Adam could easily afford to continue making his mortgage payments, he had decided to just walk away and, as he put it, let the bank deal with it.

"So what do you think?" he asked me.

I didn't hold back. "You are the all-American problem right now," I told him. "You earn plenty of money and can afford your home—yet you are letting the bank foreclose because on paper it's under water. What if I told you your house would be worth $1 million in 10 years—would you still walk away?"

"Of course not," he said, "but that will never happen."

The truth is, he doesn't know that. No one does. What we do know is that losing his home to foreclosure is going to seriously affect his credit score and potentially keep him from being able to buy a new home for years.

So if you can afford to continue making your mortgage payments, I suggest you keep making those payments and keep your house. But what if you can't?

WHAT DO YOU DO IF YOU CAN'T AFFORD TO MAKE YOUR MORTGAGE PAYMENTS?

For the past three years, millions of Americans have been in precisely this boat. The worry of losing your home can be paralyzing—but when you are faced with foreclosure, doing nothing is the biggest mistake you can make.

The good news is that there are a variety of programs designed to help people in this exact bind. Perhaps the most wide-reaching one is the federal government's Making Home Affordable program. Introduced in 2009 by the Obama administration, it aims to help as many as 9 million cash-strapped Americans by reducing their monthly mortgage payments to more affordable levels.

With this in mind, if you have a mortgage you can no longer afford and are unable to refinance, I want you to go online NOW and visit the federal government's Making Home Affordable website at **www.makinghomeaffordable.gov.**

Making Home Affordable offers two different potential solutions for borrowers: (1) the Home Affordable Refinance Program (HARP), which gives homeowners with Fannie Mae or Freddie Mac mortgages an opportunity to refinance into more affordable monthly payments; and (2) the Home Affordable Modification Program (HAMP), which has committed $75 billion to keep people in their homes by preventing avoidable foreclosures.

The easiest way to determine if you qualify for HARP is to go to the Making Home Affordable website, click on "Refinancing," and complete the four-question self-assessment. While this tool will help you determine if you are eligible, only the servicer of your loan can say for sure, so you must contact them for more information. If you are behind on your mortgage payments, you probably won't qualify for HARP. However, you may qualify for HAMP.

For more information about HAMP, go to **www.makinghomeaffordable.gov** and click on "Modification." Complete the five-question self-assessment and read through all of the FAQs. As with HARP, it's up to your mortgage servicer to decide if you're eligible. Follow the guidelines on what information you should gather before you call, then pick up the phone.

WHAT TO DO
IF YOUR LENDER WON'T HELP YOU

If you're not getting the help you need from your lender or mortgage servicer, talk to a housing counselor approved by the U.S. Department of Housing and Urban Development (HUD). He or she will help you navigate the process—free of charge. For a referral, visit the HUD website at **www.hud.gov** or call toll-free (800) 569-4287. Remember, the earlier you get help, the more options you will have and the better your chances will be to save your home.

Finally, if you need urgent help, contact the Homeowner's HOPE™ Hotline at **(888) 995-HOPE**.

HOW TO SELL
IN TODAY'S MARKET

Sometimes you have no choice: You simply cannot afford to keep your home and you have to sell. Well, don't panic. Selling a home in today's market is not easy, but it can be done.

FIVE SECRETS TO
SELLING A HOME IN TODAY'S MARKET

1. **Get professional help.** Use a top real estate agent—someone in your area who knows the local market, has the respect of other brokers, and knows what it takes to succeed in the current environment. Success speaks volumes, so you should hire the broker in your community with the best track record of selling homes over the past 12 to 18 months. Ask for proof: How many listings do they have, how long do they typically stay on the mar-

ket, how many have they sold? Focus on their results—not their "showmanship."

2. Price it right. If real estate prices are down 35% in your area and you price your home at 2007 or 2008 levels, it's simply not going to sell. Pricing a home high in the hope that you can negotiate down from there is exactly how to guarantee that nothing (no offers, no tours, no traffic) will happen. When you price a home right, it moves. There are buyers out there looking every day, and they know the market. Go to a website like www.trulia.com or www.zillow.com and get all the facts on sales in your market. A few hours on one of these sites (and a good conversation with a smart real estate agent who knows all about comparable sales in your area), and you'll have a good idea of what the right price is for your property.

3. Stage it. The fastest way to sell a home is to clean it out, paint it white, and then "stage" it—that is, hire a professional who can prepare it for showing by removing clutter and dressing up the place, often with borrowed or rented furnishings. The cost to stage a house is usually only a few thousand dollars, and it can help your home sell much faster. Trust me, what you think looks "cute" could easily turn off a buyer. You want a clean, clutter-free, neutral palette (i.e., white walls) on which a buyer can project his or her fantasies and dreams. To find a stager, ask your real estate agent for a referral or go through the International Association of Home Staging Professionals (www.iahsp.com).

4. Auction it. In the buyer's market we're currently experiencing, more and more homes are being sold through auctions. Because prices often start out way below market levels, auctions generate excitement and often provoke a ton of activity and offers in a short period of time. Most sellers use professionals to auction off their homes. You can find one who specializes in real estate through the National Auctioneers Association's real estate website at www.naarealestateauctions.com. You can also check out sites like www.bid4homes.com, www.sellwithauction.com, and www.123sold.com. (Just make sure to thoroughly check out any company you decide to do business with first.)

5. Lease it (with a purchase option). If your goal is to get out from under your mortgage because you don't have much equity in your property, then a "lease option to buy" could be a "win/win" solution for both you and a potential buyer. What you do is offer to lease your property to a tenant at a fair market rent (hopefully, one big enough to cover your mortgage payment and other expenses), and the tenant in turn gets the right to purchase the place outright at a set price sometime in the future. To sweeten the deal, if the tenant decides to buy, part of the rent he or she paid will be credited against the purchase price. For example, you rent out your condo for two years at $2,000 a month, with an agreed-upon purchase price of $200,000 and a 50% rent credit. By the end of the two-year lease, the tenant will have paid a total of $48,000 in rent—half of which (or $24,000) will be subtracted from the purchase price if he or she decides to buy, bringing their actual out-of-pocket cost down to $176,000. This can be a great deal for a buyer. And it's a great deal for you, because a tenant who is considering buying a place he is renting will probably take very good care of it.

IF YOU DON'T OWN— BUT WANT TO

I don't believe in renting long term. I want to own my own home. I want to own my office space. I like owning assets and building my net worth—and I know that the way to do this is to buy assets that will appreciate and ideally lease things that depreciate.

You need to know this too, and you need to act— because now is the time to buy. In fact, this may be the best time to buy a home that you will experience in your lifetime.

RENTING VS. OWNING: THE CHOICE IS YOURS, BUT THE OUTCOMES ARE DIFFERENT

There is a myth that over the long term, renting is cheaper than owning a home. This is just nonsense. When you rent, you are paying someone else's mortgage, property taxes, and insurance premiums, and often their management and maintenance costs as well. Think about that! No one gets into real estate to lose money. Landlords buy properties to enjoy an appreciating asset and finish rich.

So if you are renting right now because you think it's cheaper than owning, here are some facts you need to consider.

RENTS GO UP AN AVERAGE OF 4% EACH YEAR

It's a fairly safe bet that as soon as your lease expires, your rent will go up. That's just a fact of life. Overall, rents rise about 4% a year. In many markets, they climb even faster than that. This is one big reason why I believe that if you plan on living somewhere for more than a few years, it pays to own.

The fact that the price of housing has come down so significantly makes the numbers swing in favor of owning even more sharply. And that's not counting the terrific breaks homeowners get from the government. Not only does the IRS let you deduct the interest costs on mortgages of up to $1 million (plus the first $100,000 of a home-equity line), but in 2009 the government was offering a new $8,000 tax credit for first-time homebuyers (whom they define as anyone who hasn't owned a home for at least the last three years). At the time of this writing, this offer was set to expire on November 30, 2009, but chances are good that it may be extended. To find out, visit **www. irs.gov** and search for First-Time Homebuyer Credit.

Skeptics will disagree with my position on owning vs. renting, but what always amuses me is that most of these skeptics (especially those in the media) actually own their own homes. They aren't renters themselves.

HOW DO I KNOW
IF I CAN AFFORD TO OWN?

People worry about whether they can afford to buy, but let me ask you this—what makes you think you can afford to rent?

When most people are deciding whether or not to sign a lease on a place, they look at the rent figure and ask themselves, "Can I pay this and still have enough money left over to pay my other bills and not go broke?" Well, it's really no different when you own. You need to look at the monthly mortgage payment and then add on the property taxes, insurance, and maintenance costs. The result is a fixed monthly amount that represents your total cost of ownership. Once you've calculated it, you have to ask yourself whether you can afford to pay it as well as your other bills, and still be putting aside money for retirement, your emergency fund, dream accounts, and so on.

As I said earlier, your housing costs should not exceed 35% of your gross income—and, ideally, around 25%. This may mean that you have to buy less of a home than you want. That's okay—you don't always get your dream home right away. You build up to it.

I also suggest that before you buy, you have at least six months' worth of housing expenses set aside as a cushion in case you lose your job or income stream. If you don't have that much cash in the bank, you need to ramp up your savings and cut your expenses until you do, because you are not really ready to buy yet.

I'M A FIRST-TIME HOMEBUYER— HOW DO I GET FINANCING?

The good news for first-time homebuyers is that the banks are lending money again to qualified borrowers. The bad news is that credit guidelines have tightened. A lot. Even people with strong credit scores are now required to submit detailed financial documentation to receive a loan. I recently bought a new home, and I can tell you that I had to provide far more documentation to get my mortgage this time than for any loan I have ever gotten in the past.

This is the new landscape of lending. But as aggravating as it may be, I believe it's actually a good thing. The tighter lending guidelines are just what the credit markets need to regain their strength, and they will ultimately protect both homeowners and lenders going forward.

So if you want to buy a home now, don't be discouraged by all the hoops your lender makes you jump through. As I say, national banks like Wells Fargo, Bank of America, Citibank, and Chase are doing home loans every day. So pick up the phone and get the process started. The best place to begin is the bank where you already have your accounts. You can also shop for a loan online at websites like **www.bankrate.com** and **www.lendingtree.com**.

However you do it, make sure to shop for your loan BEFORE you start shopping for your home. When you start looking at houses, you already want to be PREAPPROVED for a mortgage—meaning a lender has told you in writing exactly how big a mortgage he is prepared to give you. Before preapproving you, the lender will run a credit check and ask you for documents such as recent pay stubs and bank statements to confirm you have a reliable source of income, sufficient cash for a down payment, and a big enough financial cushion to make him feel comfortable.

By getting yourself preapproved first, you can go house-hunting secure in the knowledge that if you find the right house, you will be able to get the financing you need to buy it.

One final tip: Whatever the bank says they are willing to lend you, be conservative and borrow 10% to 20% less than that.

HOW MUCH CASH WILL I NEED TO PUT DOWN TO BUY A HOME?

Warren Buffett recently said something worth repeating about homebuying. "Home purchases should involve an honest-to-God down payment of at least 10%," he wrote in his February 2009 report to the shareholders of his company, Berkshire Hathaway. I think he's right—although, in my opinion, a down payment of 20% would be even better.

That said, the reality is that you can still buy a home with as little as 3% down if you get a loan guaranteed by the Federal Housing Administration (FHA) or the Department of Veterans Affairs (VA). A VA loan is available to pretty much anyone who has served in the military and been honorably discharged. (For details on eligibility requirements, go online to **www.homeloans.va.gov/elig2.htm**.) To be eligible for an FHA loan, you must have decent (though not necessarily perfect) credit, a stable income, and be able to afford a 3% down payment. Details are available at **www.fha.gov**. (Click on the tab for "Consumers," then click the link in the left-hand column for "FHA Consumer Marketplace.")

And they *are* available. Indeed, as part of the Obama administration's economic stimulus programs, FHA loan limits were increased in 2009 to as high as $729,750 for homes in high-cost housing markets, while the VA limit runs as high as $1,094,625. You can ask your lender if you qualify for either an FHA or VA loan. For more information, visit the Federal Housing Administration's website at **www.fha.gov** or the U.S. Department of Veterans Affairs' Loan Guaranty website at **www.homeloans.va.gov**.

IS NOW A GOOD TIME TO BUY A BIGGER HOME?

Obviously, real estate markets like the one we're in now provide a phenomenal opportunity to buy your "dream home"—that is, a bigger and better home in a better neighborhood. So what's the best way to go about doing this? My recommendation is simple— find yourself a good real estate agent and go see what is out there.

But a word of caution: Unless you have enough money to carry the cost of both your old and new places, do NOT buy a new home until after you've sold your current one. *In the current market, it's a big mistake to operate on the assumption that you can easily rent out your old house to cover your expenses.* In many real estate markets these days, there is a glut of homes and apartments available, and rents may be way down. You need to look closely at the market where you are and see how much inventory there is and what places like yours are renting for.

That said, you will probably be able to find a tenant if you can afford to rent out your place at 25% below the market. In this case, you may not want to sell your old house now, but rather hang on to it until the real estate market recovers—and it will recover. The fact is that if you have the cushion and income to carry two properties comfortably, then this could be a great time for you to rent your home, buy another one to live in, and become a real estate investor. As I said, it's real estate markets like this one that provide an opportunity for average people to become millionaires.

SHOULD I INVEST IN REAL ESTATE— AND IF SO, HOW?

Let me share some super-simple and boring advice about real estate. In my experience, most people who invest successfully in real estate invest in a market they know—and this is usually their own backyard.

Chances are, if you have been in your neighborhood awhile, you know what homes are going for right now and where rents are at. So one easy way to get into the real estate investment game is to make use of this knowledge by buying a home in your neighborhood from an owner who is, as the saying goes, motivated to sell. This may be someone who is having trouble making his mortgage payments, perhaps because he's going through a divorce or has lost his job. Or maybe there's a home or condo in your neighborhood being sold by a bank through a short sale or a foreclosure sale.

As usual, the Internet is a great resource for information to get you started looking at potential investment properties. Here's a list of 10 top real-estate sites:

1. AOL Real Estate (**http://RealEstate.aol.com**)
2. Coldwell Banker (**http://ColdwellBanker.com**)
3. CyberHomes (**www.cyberhomes.com**)
4. DotHomes (**www.dothomes.com**)
5. Movoto (**www.movoto.com**)
6. National Association of Realtors (**www.Realtor .com**)
7. ReMax (**www.ReMax.com**)
8. Trulia Real Estate Search (**www.Trulia.com**)
9. Yahoo! Real Estate (**http://RealEstate.Yahoo.com**)
10. Zillow (**www.Zillow.com**)

The fact is, the landlord game is back in vogue these days because the returns from rentals are so good. Indeed, in many metropolitan markets returns are at historical highs because the price of entry is so low. People are paying so little for homes they can rent out that even with today's discounted rents, they are still earning positive cash flow.

IS NOW A GOOD TIME TO INVEST IN REAL ESTATE FUNDS?

As I write this, the market for real estate investment trusts (these are simply mutual funds that invest in real estate projects, and are better known as REITs) has jumped by more than 100% since hitting bottom back in March of 2009. That's a huge run-up. Still, as the real estate market continues to improve, I think REIT investments will ultimately go higher. Once again, I can't say where the market will be when you read this, but I like investing in REITs. They're a great way to own real estate without the bother of having to manage any properties.

My favorite way to invest in REITs is through an index fund—ideally, an exchange-traded fund (ETF) that invests in REITs. You can find a great selection at **www.ishares.com**. Clicking on the "Real Estate" tab will bring up all the real estate ETFs they manage. My favorite is the Cohen and Steers Realty Major Index

Fund (symbol: ICF). It offers a super-inexpensive way to invest in real estate that is both broadly based and extremely liquid (since you can buy and sell this fund in seconds through the stock market). Vanguard Funds (www.vanguard.com) also offers a low-cost REIT fund that I like. It's called the Vanguard REIT Index (symbol: VGSIX). The only drawback is that it requires a minimum investment of $3,000 to start.

FREE REAL ESTATE WEBISODES AT
WWW.FINISHRICH.COM

To learn more about the unprecedented opportunities in real estate these days, visit my website at www.finishrich.com. I've posted a special section on real estate, along with a series of free webisodes where I discuss real estate investing and financing. It's all there to help you—and it's free!

TO DO IN 2010 ✔

☐ Calculate your housing costs. Are you spending 25% or less of your gross income on housing? Good!

☐ Now is the time to refinance if you can find a new rate that is at least one full percentage point less than your current rate. Shop around, and stick to a plain-vanilla, fixed-rate, 30-year mortgage. Also, make sure your mortgage savings will offset the closing costs in the time you plan to own your home.

☐ If you are drowning in a mortgage you can't afford, get help. Go to www.makinghome affordable.gov, or find a housing counselor at www.hud.gov. For urgent help, call the Homeowner's HOPE Hotline at (888) 995-HOPE.

☐ Are you ready to buy? Put aside six months of housing expenses as a cushion before you take the leap.

REBUILD YOUR COLLEGE FUND (AND RESTRUCTURE YOUR STUDENT LOAN)

Even in the best of times, saving for your kids' college education can be a real challenge. In the aftermath of the worst economic turmoil in 75 years, it can seem downright impossible. Not only is it tougher than ever to scrape together enough cash to keep your college savings plan properly funded, but any money you already managed to put aside probably suffered the same kind of meltdown as your 401(k) or IRA account.

But just as with your retirement saving, the fact that the economy has done a number on your college fund doesn't mean you should give up on it. Believe me when I tell you that you *can* regain the ground you lost and put yourself on a more secure path to fully funding your children's education. And in this step I'll show you how.

IF YOU'VE GOT COLLEGE-BOUND KIDS, YOU DEFINITELY NEED A SAVINGS PLAN

One thing the recession hasn't changed is the fact that higher education is a dauntingly expensive proposition. And it's getting more expensive with every passing year. According to the College Board, the bill for a typical four-year private-college education currently runs around $130,000; for state schools, the figure is roughly $54,000. By 2024, says the College Savings Foundation, the cost of a four-year college education will likely total more than $200,000 at a private institution and more than $100,000 at a public college.

So unless you're rolling in dough, if you have kids and want to send them to college, you will definitely need to have a savings plan. Sure, there are scholarships and student loans, but the odds that they will cover all your costs (or even most of them) are increasingly long.

The good news is that there is a variety of programs designed to help you save for college—including a wide assortment of government-sponsored savings programs known as 529 savings plans that allow you to put away as much as $300,000 or more on a tax-deferred basis. The bad news is that when the stock market nosedived in 2008–09, so did most people's college savings. As of the first quarter of 2008, parents of college-bound kids had invested nearly $109 billion in 529 accounts. A year later, the value of those assets had dropped by more than 20%, to an estimated $85.9 billion.

Not surprisingly, this spooked a lot of college savers. Between the first quarter of 2008 and the first quarter of 2009, the amount of new money invested in 529 accounts plummeted by nearly 40%.

Some of this decrease was probably the result of people simply not being able to afford to continue making contributions to their college funds. But a lot of people were clearly scared off by the big stock market declines. According to a Gallup survey commissioned by Sallie Mae, the nation's biggest provider of student loans, nearly 60% of the people saving for college in 2009 avoided 529 plans and instead put their money into regular savings accounts, money-market accounts, or bank certificates of deposit.

I hope you weren't one of them. The fact is, you can invest your money every bit as safely in a 529 plan as you can anywhere else—plus there are tremendous advantages to using a 529 plan that you don't get with a savings account, money-market account, or bank CD.

WHAT MAKES 529 PLANS
SUCH A GREAT DEAL

Like 401(k)s, 529 plans get their name from the section of the tax code that authorizes them. Formally known as qualified tuition programs, they are by far the best way to save for college. Every state has its own rules for 529 plans, but they all fall into one of two categories: They are either prepaid tuition programs that let you lock in the cost of your child's future college education at today's prices, or they are savings plans that let you set up a tax-deferred savings account on your kid's behalf.

Some 19 states offer section 529 prepaid tuition programs, under which you can pay for all or part of your child's college education now—at current rates—even though he or she may not be attending college for another 10 or 15 years. Some prepaid plans allow you to purchase individual tuition credits. Others let you prepay anywhere from one to five years' worth of tuition for each child. You can do this either with a lump-sum payment or on an installment plan.

Every state except Washington offers 529 college savings plans. As with 401(k) accounts or IRAs, the contributions you make to a 529 savings plan are usually invested in mutual funds or similar securities. (Also like a 401(k), most 529 savings plans offer a menu of funds for you to choose from.) The nice thing is that you can put in just about as much money as you want (more than $300,000 in some plans), as long as the amount doesn't exceed your child's eventual college costs. And while the federal government doesn't let you deduct 529 contributions from your taxes, many state governments do. What's more, your money can grow tax-free as long as it stays in the account—and no taxes are due when you withdraw the money, as long as it's spent on qualified college expenses.

The biggest drawback of 529 savings plans is that if the funds are used for some purpose other than qualified education expenses—say, because you saved too much or because your kid decided not to go to college—they will be subject to taxes *and* a 10% penalty. Then again, it's easy to move 529 plans from one beneficiary to another. So if your child drops off the college track, you can transfer the account to a sibling—or even a parent or other close relative.

CHOOSING THE RIGHT 529 PLAN

With dozens of different college savings plans to choose from, picking the right one was a challenge even before the recession. Fortunately, informational websites like Bankrate's **SavingforCollege.com** and the investment site Morningstar (www.morningstar.com) regularly post lists of the best 529 plans. The Savingfor- College list compares fees, whereas the Morningstar rankings consider fund diversification as well. Another good resource is the College Savings Plan Network, an organization of state officials who administer 529 plans. Its website (www.collegesavings.org) offers comprehensive information about every 529 plan in the nation and allows you to make side-by-side com- parisons.

In Morningstar's 2009 survey, the top five 529 plans were:

1. Ohio CollegeAdvantage (managed by Ohio Tu- ition Trust Authority)
2. Indiana CollegeChoice 529 Direct Savings Plan (Upromise Investments)
3. Utah Educational Savings Plan Trust (UESP Trust)
4. Virginia Education Savings Trust (Virginia Col- lege Savings Plan Board)
5. Virginia CollegeAmerica 529 Savings Plan (American Funds)

FIVE THINGS
YOU SHOULD DO DIFFERENTLY NOW

As I've said a number of times in this book, recession or no, the basic rules of finishing rich haven't changed. But this doesn't mean the recent economic turmoil hasn't taught us anything new. Certainly, when it comes to saving for college, there are a few things we should probably be doing differently now. Here are the top five.

1. Save for college after you've funded your emergency account and your retirement plan. The single biggest mistake most parents make when it comes to college savings is making Junior's college funding too much of a priority. Saving for your kids' education is important, but you should *not* put it ahead of your own emergency or retirement needs. Even paying off high-interest debt should get priority over college savings. Why? Because while you can borrow for college, you can't borrow for those other things.

2. Make sure your plan isn't too aggressive. When it comes to balancing growth potential against risk, college savings plans are very much like retirement plans. In both cases, it's fine to be aggressive and take risks in the early years in order to achieve high returns. But as the target date approaches (whether you're looking at retirement or freshman enrollment), your asset allocation should gradually become more conservative, moving away from riskier investments like stocks and toward safer ones like bonds and cash. Most experts agree that a good college savings plan should start reducing the proportion invested in stocks when your child is around 13; by the time he or she turns 17 (the year before college), the stock allocation should be down to less than 25%. So visit your plan's website and check out its asset-allocation strategy; if it's too aggressive for too long, find another plan.

3. Pay closer attention. When markets are volatile, the automatic rebalancing strategies that most 529 plans follow can get you in trouble. Specifically, while it certainly makes sense to reduce your stock holdings as your child approaches college age, if the market is tanking, selling stocks at that point will only lock in losses. As one expert told **Bankrate.com:** "The idea that you can park your money and not worry about it doesn't work. You need to examine your college funds periodically." In particular, you want to make sure that the investment option you chose still makes sense in light of whatever is going on with the economy at that particular moment. If it doesn't, think about switching to a different option within your plan.

4. Be wary of prepaid-tuition plans. When they work, prepaid-tuition plans can be good deals, but as a consequence of the 2008–09 stock market meltdown—plus the never-ending wave of tuition increases—many are on shaky ground right now. After the downturn left Alabama's prepaid-tuition fund with less than half the money it needs to pay future tuition commitments, the state closed its program to new savers. West Virginia's prepaid-tuition program is in a similar boat, with an $8 million shortfall due to investment losses. As of the summer of 2009, only seven states (Florida, Maryland, Massachusetts, Mississippi, Texas, Virginia, and Washington) were promising to bail out their tuition programs if money ran short—but there was no guarantee that they would stick to that promise. So for the time being I would think twice before going the prepaid route.

5. Don't assume you have to do it all yourself. Parents aren't the only ones who can contribute to a 529 plan. Grandparents can too—and in one recent survey, some 60% of grandparents said they would be happy to do so if they were asked. You can also register with GradeFund (**www.gradefund.com**), a website through which students can raise money for education costs by recruiting friends, family, and organizations to sponsor their drive for good grades. (You upload your academic transcript to the site, and in return for achieving targeted performance levels, you get cash rewards.) Another helpful website is Sallie Mae's Upromise (**www.upromise.com**), where you can sign up for free to earn cash-back rewards of up to 25% when you shop at any one of 600 online retailers, 8,000 restaurants, or 21,000 grocery and drug stores. The money you save can be used to fund a 529 account, pay off an existing Sallie Mae student loan, or pay college expenses. This is no gimmick. Since launching in 2001, Upromise has enrolled 10 million members and paid out more than $500 million in member rewards.

WHAT TO DO IF YOU CAN'T PAY YOUR STUDENT LOAN

When it comes to college finances, older people generally worry about how they're going to afford to pay their kids' tuition bills. Younger people have a more immediate concern. The question I hear most often from them is: "What do I do about my student loan?"

Given how hard it's been lately for recent graduates to find good jobs, it's hardly surprising that the default rate for student loans has been soaring. In 2007, only about one out of every 20 new borrowers failed to make his or her student loan payments. In 2008, the figure jumped to one out of every 14 borrowers (or more than 230,000 in all). And this was before the worst effects of the recession really began to be felt.

So if you're having problems keeping up with your student loan payments, you're not alone. Does this make you feel better? I didn't think it would. But here's something that should: There is a long list of things you can do to make your student-debt burden lighter—and maybe even go away entirely.

In most cases, there's really only one thing you need to do to get a break on your student loan: You've got to be totally straight with your lender. If you start missing payments without saying anything to your lender, there's no end to the bad things that might happen to you: delinquency, default, a ruined credit rating, having your wages garnished, maybe even getting sued. On the other hand, if you let your lender know up front that you've got a problem, you'd be amazed how many options you have and how willing he will likely be to work something out with you.

SWITCH TO
AN EASIER REPAYMENT PLAN

Once you've informed your lender that you may have trouble making your payments, the first thing you should do is find out if you can switch to an easier repayment plan. The standard student-loan repayment plan is 120 equal payments once a month for ten years. But that's not chiseled in stone. Both the federal government and private lenders that make government-guaranteed loans offer a variety of payment plans. If you meet certain criteria, you can generally switch to a more manageable plan without hurting your credit score. The main alternatives include:

Extended repayment. If your student-loan debt totals more than $30,000, you can extend your repayment period to anywhere from 12 to 30 years, which will reduce your monthly payment. Of course, since you continue paying interest until your entire debt is repaid, the longer you stretch it out, the more money your loan will wind up costing you.

Graduated repayment. As with the extended plan, your loan term is stretched out to as much as 30 years. But instead of reducing your monthly payment by the same small amount for the entire time, graduated repayment cuts it by as much as 50% for the first few years. After this initial period, the monthly payment is then increased every two years for the remainder of the loan term (though it can never total more than 150% of the standard monthly payment).

Income-contingent repayment. Meant for students who go into public service or other lower-paying pursuits, income-contingent repayment bases your monthly payment on a variety of factors, including annual income and family size. If your income is so low that you still owe money after 25 years, the outstanding balance will be forgiven.

Income-sensitive repayment. Similar to the income-contingent repayment, income-sensitive repayment is a short-term alternative for low-income borrowers who've gotten government-guaranteed student loans from private lenders through the Federal Family Education Loan Program. Under it, your monthly payment is set somewhere between 4% and 25% of your gross monthly income. Your loan term remains ten years, so the longer you continue on this plan, the higher your payments for the rest of the term will be.

Income-based repayment. Also meant for low-income borrowers, income-based repayment limits monthly payments to no more than 15% of a borrower's discretionary income, which is defined as any earnings above 150% of the poverty line. In 2009, this would have been anything above $16,000 a year for a single person. (For example, if your annual income was $20,000 in 2009, your discretionary income would have been $4,000, and the maximum loan payment you'd have to make would have been 15% of that, which works out to $50 a month.) Borrowers who earn less than $16,000—or whatever 150% of the poverty line happens to be in a given year—don't have to pay anything. As with income-contingent repayment, the maximum loan term is 25 years; after that, any remaining debt is forgiven.

IF YOU CAN'T PAY ANYTHING, YOU MIGHT BE ABLE TO DEFER

Reduced payments aren't much help if you're totally broke. Fortunately, the student loan system is designed to cut you slack even if you can't afford to make any payments at all right now.

Once again, the key is being straight with your lender. If you've borrowed directly from the government and you notify them BEFORE you default, you may be able to get a deferment, which allows you to put off making payments for as long as three years without incurring any interest charges or damaging your credit record. To be eligible, you must be able to prove economic hardship (both the inability to find full-time employment and military service qualify as good reasons).

If you've borrowed from a private lender (or don't meet the requirements for a deferment), you might be able to get your lender to give you what's called a forbearance, where he agrees to let you suspend making payments for up to a year. The catch here is that during the suspension period you do incur interest charges, which will be added to your loan balance.

AND YOU MIGHT EVEN GET OFF THE HOOK ENTIRELY!

If none of these options work for you—or if you've used them up and still can't meet your obligations—you may have a chance to get your student loan forgiven entirely. There are a number of federal and state programs under which certain borrowers who've pursued such public service–oriented careers as teaching, nursing, law enforcement, or the military can get their loans canceled outright. For details, talk to your HR department, union, or professional association. For example, the American Federation of Teachers maintains a list of loan-forgiveness programs for teachers.

A number of volunteer organizations, such as AmeriCorps, the Peace Corps, and VISTA, have their own loan-forgiveness programs, as do the Army National Guard and numerous medical, nursing, and physical-therapy associations. The rules vary widely; in some cases, you have to make at least ten years' worth of payments before a loan can be forgiven, while in others you can have 70% of your loan canceled immediately.

Finally, if you already have defaulted, don't give up. Call your lender and see if you can work something out. Defaults benefit no one, and in some cases, a lender may be willing to reinstate you if you prove your reliability by resuming payment and going ten months or so without missing a deadline.

MAKE AN INVESTMENT IN YOURSELF

Yes, higher education is more expensive than ever. But as the economy changes, education is one of the best investments you can make. It can help you grow your income and reach your full potential as a human being. So don't let the high cost thwart your ambitions. Instead, use the strategies in this chapter to make your dreams come true.

TO DO IN 2010 ✔

☐ 529 plans are the best way to save for college.

☐ Make sure your plan is not too aggressive. It should start shifting away from stocks when your child is 13 and that stock allocation should be down to less than 25% by the time he or she is 17.

☐ Monitor your plan's automatic rebalancing strategy.

☐ If you are struggling to repay your student loan, stop struggling. Instead, investigate the wide range of options you have to renegotiate your payments.

25 WAYS
TO SAVE $5,000

You have come a long way in your "Start Over" Action Plan—but we are not done yet! This step is easy and really important because a great way to jump-start your plan is to cut your overhead, at least for a short time, and put the savings back in your pocket. In this step, I'm going to share with you 25 ways to cut your expenses by $5,000 in 2010. In fact, if you were to implement all 25 steps, you'd wind up saving more than *$15,000* by the end of the year! Some of these steps are so simple that they are truly no-brainers. Others require a little more commitment and effort, and a few require some planning ahead on your part.

See how many steps you can complete and how much cash you will save. This one step could save you at least 10 times the cost of this book—and more than likely 100 times what you paid. Now that's a great investment!

So let's get started—and have some fun starting over and finishing rich!

1. Lose the premium cable TV package . . . and save $600.

The average premium cable TV package—the one that offers more than 200 channels and first-run movies—can easily cost $100 a month when you include the charges for the cable boxes, DVR, remote controls, and all the crazy taxes and unexplainable expenses that are legally tacked onto your bill. That's $1,200 a year just to watch TV!

In fact, you probably only watch maybe a dozen of those 200 channels. Do you really need all the extra ones? And do you really need a recording feature on every TV in your house? (You know you're paying for that, right?) If you downgrade to a more basic cable package (many of which start at just $19.99 a month) and stop paying for DVR features you don't use and remotes you don't need (yes, you're also paying for remotes you don't use—check your bill), you could easily cut your bill by at least $50 per month, or about $600 a year—and possibly even more.

☐ TAKE ACTION: Pull out your cable bill. Determine what you're spending now and for what. Then call your provider to ask about downgrade options. Can't negotiate a better deal? Then switch to a new cable service or direct satellite TV. The competition among providers is fierce, so you should be able to cut your costs here in minutes. I reduced my cable bill by nearly $80 a month when I did this—that's over $900 a year I am saving now, and you can do it too!

2. Get real about your cell phone . . . and save $240.

According to a recent study by the Utility Consumers' Action Network, the average cell phone customer uses only one-third of the total minutes he or she purchases each month! So chances are that you could get by with a much cheaper cell phone plan than you've currently got.

Right now, an individual 900-minute plan from Verizon Wireless costs $60 a month. Add in taxes and fees, and you're looking at a monthly bill of at least $80—or close to $1,000 a year in cell phone charges. If you switch to a plan that offers, say, 450 minutes, it will cost you only $40 a month, or $60 including taxes and fees. That's a savings of $20 a month, or $240 a year. And considering all the available bells and whistles, chances are that your cell phone bill is higher than what I figured in my example above— meaning you could probably save even more by downgrading.

□ TAKE ACTION: When was the last time you reviewed your cell phone usage? Pull out your bill and call your carrier today. Have them look at your records for the last six months and, based on your usage, choose a plan that better fits your needs. After you've figured out what your current carrier can save you, go online to **www.billshrink.com** and see what the competition has to offer. Then go with whoever has the best deal.

3. Ditch your landline . . . and save $240.

More and more people are canceling their landline phone service altogether and using a cell phone in place of a regular home phone. Your landline probably costs you at least $20 a month, so discontinuing it would mean a savings of at least $240 a year. At a minimum, downgrade your landline service to the most basic level. My "basic plan" was costing me more than $70 a month . . . until I called the phone company and hammered them to really give me the most basic plan. This saved me $40 a month. If you get great cell phone reception at home, are organized enough not to lose your phone, and are good about keeping it charged, this might be a great solution for you.

□ **TAKE ACTION:** Call your local phone company and cancel your landline service, or downgrade to a basic package.

4. Bundle your telecom services . . . and save $1,500.

Let's say you don't feel comfortable getting rid of your landline and you're a big telecom user—that is, someone who regularly phones all over the country, is used to watching a lot more than basic cable, and needs the speed of a broadband Internet connection. If this describes you, then bundling can deliver real value.

Bundling simply means that you purchase all three home telecom services—phone, Internet, and cable TV—from the same company (a "triple play" in the industry's jargon) for one price. The competition for bundled customers is so stiff that many companies offer very low introductory rates. Just make sure you know how long that rate will last and how much it will go up after the initial period ends.

My friend Allan spends about $150 a month on phone service through Verizon, $175 on cable TV service from Charter, and $50 a month on high-speed Internet service through Earthlink—for a total of $375 per month. If he got all those services through Verizon, which offers a variety of bundled packages, it would cost him just $250 a month. So bundling could save him $1,500 a year!

☐ TAKE ACTION: Call your phone carrier and cable company to find out how much you could save by bundling your phone, Internet, and cable TV services.

5. Exercise smart . . . and save $600.

We all know the trap: You sign up for a gym membership and you wind up going a lot less often than you thought you would. It happens all the time.

I have friends who belong to gyms that cost them $100 or more a month, and they never go.

One solution is to see if you can downgrade to a more basic membership. This can save you at least $20 a month, or $240 a year. Better still, trade in your membership altogether for a pair of running shoes and save about $50 a month—or $600 a year!

☐ **Take Action:** If you use your gym, phone them today and let them know that if you can't get a better price on your membership, you will need to cancel it. Often, just making this call can get you a better deal. Don't worry if they won't budge. With new customers increasingly hard to come by, everyone is offering great deals, which makes this a great time to switch gym memberships. And if you don't use your gym, then cancel your membership today.

6. Shop your car insurance . . . and save $600.

This one's a no-brainer. If you own or lease a car, car insurance is a must-have. But you can't settle for the first rate quote you get—you've got to shop around. Simply by picking up the phone and comparing quotes, you could wind up saving 10% to 15% on what you're paying now, possibly more.

My assistant saved $800 with a 10-minute phone call. Yes, that sounds like a line from a commercial, but it's the truth! Even with a more conservative estimate of, say, $600 a year, it's still a windfall.

☐ **TAKE ACTION:** The Internet has made every

insurance company more competitive—so get online and shop those rates! Visit the major carriers' sites, such as **www.geico.com, www.allstate.com, www.progressive.com, www.statefarm.com,** and **www.nationwide.com.** In addition, check out comparison sites like **www.netquote.com, www.insurance.com, www.insure.com,** and **www.esurance.com.** Then call your carrier. Tell him to beat the best price you found or you'll take your business elsewhere. You're in the driver's seat, so make that call.

One other tip: The fastest way to cut your car insurance premiums is to increase your deductible. In most cases, hiking your deductible by $500 to $1,000 will lower your premiums by 10% or more. Also, if you don't rack up a lot of miles, check out Progressive's MyRate plan (**www.progressive.com**). This is a pay-as-you-drive program that bases your premium on how much you drive. The less you drive, the less you pay.

7. Shop for your homeowner's insurance . . . and save $480.

In many areas around the country this past year, the cost of homeowner's insurance jumped sharply. But this doesn't mean you have to accept a new, higher rate. As with car insurance, you can use the power of the Internet to get yourself a better deal.

When it comes to getting the best rate, be aware that:

- You should be insuring only your house, not the land it sits on.
- You pay less if you have security systems and fire alarms in place.
- You pay less if you're a nonsmoker.
- You may qualify for a discount if you have recently renovated your electrical, heating, and/or plumbing systems.
- You can get a discount if you buy your homeowner's insurance from the same company that insures your car.

☐ TAKE ACTION: Go online and shop around. Have a copy of your current policy available so you know what's included in your current coverage. Visit sites like **www.insuranceagents.com**, **www.netquote. com**, **www.accuqote.com**, and **www.insureme.com**. If you have an insurance agent, call him or her as well. Once you have competitive quotes, call your current carrier to see if they will match or beat them. Also, just as with car insurance, another super-fast way to lower your rates is to raise your deductible. Ask your carrier how much you would need to raise your deductible in order to save 20%. If it's an amount you think you could handle, then go for it!

8. Shop for your life insurance . . . and save $500.

While you're comparison shopping for a better auto or homeowner's policy, don't forget about life insurance! In recent years, life insurance premiums have come down between 20% and 50%. So if you haven't shopped for a new rate recently, you may be in for a pleasant surprise—especially if you don't smoke and you've been healthy for the last 12 to 24 months.

☐ **TAKE ACTION:** Get competitive quotes from websites such as **www.findmyinsurance.com, www. lifeinsure.com,** and **www.accuquote.com,** then call your current carrier and ask them to match or beat the best new quote you found. You're likely to save at least $500 a year.

9. Cancel your subscriptions . . . and save $400.

Between magazines, newspapers, and other home-delivered goods and services like Netflix, you could be spending well over $400 a year on subscriptions. Premium Netflix service costs $17 a month—and if you're like many people, you hold on to the same DVDs for weeks at a time. Consider downgrading to a cheaper plan or cancel the service altogether. The same goes for magazines and newspapers. Instead of paying for home delivery, consider all the free content available online now.

☐ **TAKE ACTION:** Gather up all your subscriptions, pick up the phone, and cancel them. You'll find that you're able to put about $400 back in your pocket. Also—trust me on this—the moment you cancel a subscription, you will start getting offers to resubscribe at half the price you were paying.

10. Lower your credit card interest rates and eliminate fees ... and save $475.

. In 2007, interest charges paid by U.S. credit card holders totaled $116 billion! As I often say, it's not the actual debt that is killing us—it's the interest that we're paying on that debt. Take the following example: If you're carrying a $5,000 balance on a card that charges you 23% interest, you'll pay $645 in finance charges if you pay off the balance within a year. Negotiate that rate down to 10%, and you'll pay only $275 interest—a savings of $370.

Now look at the unnecessary fees you might be paying. Do you ever get hit with late charges (which average $34 a month) or over-the-limit fees (they average $37 a month)? Pay late just twice a year and go over the limit just once and that's an easy $105 in extra fees you've just been hit with.

□ TAKE ACTION: Turn to page 46 in Step 3 of this book and find the section titled "How to Get Your Interest Rates Lowered." There you'll find my advice and instructions on how to effectively negotiate a lower rate with your credit card company. Once you've completed this step, then commit to staying below your limit and set up automatic payments to ensure you never pay a bill late again—because once you do, the low interest rate you initially received will start to skyrocket. Finally, check your statements for the past six months to see if you've been charged any penalty fees (such as over-the-limit or late-payment fees). If you have and your account is current, ask the credit card company to credit you back those fees. In many cases, they will do so on the spot, especially if you point out nicely that you are paying your bills on time and have been a loyal customer.

11. Stop paying debit card and ATM fees ... and save $98.

Americans use debit cards to purchase more than $1 trillion worth of goods each year; they account for two-thirds of all Visa transactions and half of Visa's dollar volume. The problem is that debit cards can cost you big-time if you're not careful. All told, the banks collect close to $9 billion a year in overdraft fees resulting from careless debit card use. So make sure you know what your available balance is *before* you use your debit card. Exceeding your balance just twice a month can cost you $68.

Even if you're careful not to incur overdraft fees, you can still rack up usage fees that really add up over time. How often have you made an ATM withdrawal where you're charged a $3 fee just to take money out of your own account? Use a "foreign" ATM just 10 times each month and you've just spent $30 that you didn't have to.

☐ **TAKE ACTION**: Pull out your bank statement and tally up what you're spending each month on debit card and ATM fees. Find out what your bank charges you every time you use your debit or ATM card. Visit sites like **www.findabetterbank.com** or **www.bank rate.com** to find a bank that doesn't charge you for using their own ATMs and then commit to using only their machines to withdraw money. Better yet, find a bank that actually gives you a credit for any ATM and debit card fees you incur (I personally save more than $200 a year as a result of my bank and this feature).

12. Cash in your points . . . and save $200.

If you're like me, you earn points through a variety of different rewards programs—by using certain credit cards or via frequent-flyer programs or other customer-loyalty plans. Don't let those points go unused! Very often, you can use customer-loyalty points (or miles) on a wide variety of purchases. At **www.visaextras.com,** you can enroll your eligible Visa card and earn points that can be used for back-to-school shopping, appliances, furniture, clothing—even food—at more than 150 participating companies. (Note: Some card issuers charge you to participate, so be sure to check when you enroll online.)

☐ **TAKE ACTION**: Call your credit card companies and airlines and get an up-to-date statement of how many points or miles you have accumulated. I recently did this and discovered 725,000 unused points in one of my frequent-flyer programs! (I'm now planning to go to the South of France for free with these points.) If you're not earning points on purchases you make with your current credit card, be sure to call your credit card company or bank and find out how to get enrolled in a program where you are. The same applies for travel. If you fly a lot, be sure you're enrolled in your favorite airline's frequent-flyer program as well as the preferred-guest programs at your favorite hotels. And don't leave money on the table. Redeem what you've earned.

13. Carpool to work . . . and save $382.

An astonishing 91% of Americans commute to work alone in their cars, averaging 30 miles per round-trip. As I write this in the summer of 2009, the average cost of gas is $2.65 per gallon. So if you carpooled to work just twice a week, you could save yourself $382 a year—and that's just on gas alone, not including any parking fees, tolls, or similar expenses.
□ **Take Action:** Connect with a car pool, or start one yourself by visiting **www.erideshare.com** or **www.car poolworld.com**.

14. Have a garage sale . . . and earn $210.

You may no longer want your old couch or coffeemaker, but someone else will! Selling your used stuff—whether through eBay, Craigslist, or an old-fashioned garage sale—is a great way to pocket some extra cash. People traded $52 billion worth of items last year on eBay! That's $210 per user!

☐ **TAKE ACTION:** Set up an eBay account (**www.ebay.com**) and start selling your unwanted stuff. Or visit **www.craigslist.org** and post your items there. For great tips on how to have a profitable yard sale, visit **www.yardsalequeen.com**. Also, take your clothes to a consignment shop—and pocket the cash once they sell your clothes for you. Check Google online in your area for consignment shops and visit a few—many even pay you in advance of the sale of your clothes.

15. Lower your utility bill with a free energy audit . . . and save $360.

Don't waste your money on high energy bills. Many utility companies offer some type of energy audit at no (or very low) cost. The results of an energy audit can lead you to make changes that will save as much as 30% on your utility bills! Very often, a few simple low-cost preventative actions can start reducing your bill immediately.

Sealing leaks and adding insulation where needed are the cheapest and quickest energy improvements you can make to your home. In fact, according to the Environmental Protection Agency, fixing poor insulation and reducing drafts and other air leaks can save you up to 20% on your utility bills. If your electric bill currently runs $150 a month, that's a savings of $360 a year.

My friend Liz made a concerted effort to cut her electric bill by hanging her laundry out to dry in the summer, keeping the thermostat set high, and changing the furnace filter regularly. As a result, her monthly bill dropped by $55. Total annual savings: $660.

□ **TAKE ACTION**: Call your local utility company today to ask what kind of audits they can do for you. You can also try the do-it-yourself audits available through **www.energystar.gov** and from the Consumer's Guide to Energy Efficiency at **www.eere.energy.gov**.

16. Buy in bulk . . . and save $400.

Buying in bulk doesn't mean purchasing large cases of individually wrapped goods, and it certainly doesn't mean buying things you don't really need because you couldn't resist the bargain. Buying in bulk means buying the largest size of a product that you were going to purchase anyway. The largest size almost always costs less per unit—often much less.

□ **TAKE ACTION**: The bulk-bin aisle at your supermarket is a great place to start. You can dispense dry goods like pasta, rice, cereal, nuts, dried fruit, and spices into your own bags at much lower prices per unit. Some stores also sell bulk liquids such as cooking oil, soap, shampoo, and lotion in a similar fashion.

Join a bulk-buying club or co-op where you can purchase larger-size containers of almost anything you use in your home. Costco (www.costco.com) and Sam's Club (www.samsclub.com) are two great options. Join with a friend, split your purchases, and save even more.

17. Take a volunteer vacation . . . and save $3,000.

Taking the average family of four to the archetypical American vacation spot—Disney World—can cost $5,000 to $6,000 or more by the time you figure in the cost for flights, food, lodging, park admission, and all the goodies. Now, I love theme parks and relaxation as much as the next person. But this year, consider doing something a little different. Cut the cost of getting away by giving some time to a good cause by taking a volunteer vacation. You'll likely spend far less—and you will see and experience far more than you would on a typical camping trip, cruise, or resort stay. Volunteer vacations combine travel, relaxation, and meaningful "together time" with exciting, educational experiences offered by a wide range of nonprofit organizations doing good work in the United States and abroad.

The benefits of volunteer vacations go well beyond just having a good time. You'll end up with memories, stories, and friendships that will last a lifetime. You'll also learn new skills and discover new interests that will enrich your life. And you may well have a life-changing experience that gives you a new focus or purpose—all for a fraction of the cost of a typical vacation.

☐ **Take Action:** Check out a variety of websites to choose a volunteer vacation that's right for you: These include **www.charityguide.org**, **www.transitions abroad.com**, **www.earthwatch.org**, **www.globalvolunteers.org**, and **www.travelocity.com/travelforgood**.

18. Bring your lunch to work . . . and save $2,250.

For years, my Grandmother Rose Bach brownbagged her lunch when she worked at Gimbel's department store. She invested the money she saved from not eating out and became a millionaire! Today, Americans spend more than $134 billion a year on fast food. While it's convenient, it's not always cheap (or healthy). Let's say you spend $9 every day on lunch at your local deli. That's $45 a week—or $2,250 a year! If you were to save that amount every year and invest it, in 20 years you'd have more than $111,000!

☐ **TAKE ACTION:** Cook a little extra at dinnertime, put the leftovers into single-serving-size containers, and store them in the freezer. Take one to work every day for lunch.

19. Telecommute to work . . . and save $430.

More people are working from home than ever before, and both employers and employees are reaping the rewards. By telecommuting just two days per week, an employee will drive 3,000 fewer miles and save approximately $430 in gas over the course of a year—probably more if you factor in tolls, parking, and car maintenance.

☐ TAKE ACTION: If telecommuting makes sense for the job you do, ask your employer for a trial program. Let your boss know that in addition to saving you money, telecommuting will benefit the company by reducing office space requirements, operating expenses, absenteeism, and turnover, while increasing employee productivity.

For suggestions on how to present a proposal, read "Making Your Case for Telecommuting" at **www.quintcareers.com/telecommuting_options.html**. For research to support your case, visit the website of the nonprofit Telework Coalition at **www.telcoa. org**.

20. Get your 401(k) match . . . and earn $1,480.

If you have a 401(k) retirement plan at work and you are not enrolled, you are walking away from a pile of free money. Many employers will match up to 50% of your contributions—and as of 2009, you could contribute up to $16,500 a year to a 401(k) plan ($22,000, if you were over 50). This means your company could be kicking in as much as $8,250. The most common employer matching contribution has a ceiling of 3% to 4% of a participant's pay. If you make the average American salary of $37,000 per year, that's $1,480 extra you could be earning.

☐ TAKE ACTION: Call your human resources department today to find out what your company match is—then start contributing to your 401(k) plan. If you're already enrolled, make sure you're "maxing out" your contribution.

21. Freelance . . . and earn $1,000.

What talent or job skill do you have that would allow you to do some freelancing on the side— maybe even just one weekend a month? Are you a skilled copywriter, editor, or bookkeeper? Maybe you're a fabulous cook or graphic designer? Whether it's mowing lawns, tutoring, or babysitting, people are always willing to pay for great service.

☐ TAKE ACTION: Visit sites like **www.elance.com, www.guru.com,** or **www.craigslist.org** to list your services. Alternatively, you could simply post some flyers at your local library, supermarket, or church.

22. Reclaim abandoned property . . . and earn $250.

Did you know that state treasurers and other government agencies in the United States and Canada are currently sitting on nearly $33 billion in unclaimed or abandoned property? Some of it could be yours. Unclaimed property refers to accounts in financial institutions and companies that haven't been used in at least a year or where the owner hasn't been heard from for more than a year. Common forms of unclaimed property include savings or checking accounts, stocks, uncashed dividends or payroll checks, refunds, traveler's checks, unredeemed money orders or gift certificates, insurance payments or refunds, security deposits, and contents of safe-deposit boxes. Experts estimate that one out of every eight people has money coming to them from unclaimed property sitting in some government file. The average claim is $250, but you'd be surprised how many people collect much more than that.

□ TAKE ACTION: Visit the website of the National Administration of Unclaimed Property Administrators at www.unclaimed.org and look up your name and the states in which you've resided. It takes just a few minutes, and you never know what you might find! While you're on the site, click on "Other Sources for Unclaimed Property" for a more extensive search.

23. Renegotiate your rent . . . and save $500.

Earlier I mentioned that on average rents increase about 4% a year. However, as a result of the recession, some markets have seen a decrease in rent prices. In these markets, landlords are desperate to attract and keep good tenants—which means that if you're a renter and it's time to renew your lease, your landlord may be willing to lower the rent. In an effort to keep their buildings rented, many New York City landlords are offering discounts of up to 20% to renewing tenants. Even if your lease isn't up, there are so many great bargains to be had in most major cities that you may be able to break your lease, lose your deposit, and still come out ahead.

□ **TAKE ACTION:** Do your homework on where rents are in your neighborhood right now. Use online rent-comparison tools like Rentometer (**www.rentometer.com**) and Zilpy (**www.zilpy.com**) to compare your current rent with that of other local properties. Provide your landlord or building manager with concrete examples in order to build your case. An excellent payment history on your part will certainly help as well.

24. Drive smart . . . and save $798.

No matter what kind of car you drive, maintaining it so it runs at peak efficiency is just common sense—the kind of sense that adds up to dollars. Having your tires inflated to the right pressure can increase your gas mileage by up to 3%. Installing a clean air filter protects your engine and can increase your fuel economy by another 10% or more. On the other hand, aggressive driving and braking can reduce your highway mileage by a third. Driving too fast can cost you 20 cents per gallon of gas for every 5 mph you speed over 60 mph. Finally, don't haul around unnecessary cargo. This weighs down your car and reduces your mpg.

☐ TAKE ACTION: Calculate your savings. The Department of Energy's Fuel Economy website shows exactly how much you can save per gallon of gas just by keeping your car well maintained and driving efficiently. Go to **www.fueleconomy.gov** and click on "Gas Mileage Tips." Then call your mechanic for a tune-up.

25. Stop playing Lotto . . . and save $500.

Despite the ridiculous odds against winning, Americans spent an estimated $57 billion on lottery tickets in 2006, or roughly $500 per household, according to the National Association of State and Provincial Lotteries. Playing the lottery is a waste of time and money. It is not a strategy for creating wealth.

☐ TAKE ACTION: Before you buy your next lottery ticket, read what the odds against winning are. Then tuck those bills back in your wallet.

RIGHT NOW—MAKE A PHONE CALL!

Did you just flip through this chapter—or have you already started implementing these money-saving tips? If you have already started—and you have made some significant savings—please do me and your

fellow readers a favor. Go to www.facebook.com/
DavidBach and post a success story. Your success
story could convince another reader like you to take
the same action you did.

If you haven't taken any action yet, then do yourself a favor and pick three things from this chapter
that you can do this week. Then pick one that you
will do RIGHT NOW!

Below is a worksheet to help you make the decision.

START OVER SAVING ACTION FORM

TODAY, I WILL TAKE THE FOLLOWING ACTION
TO SAVE MONEY:

1. _____

_____

_____

_____

_____

THIS WEEK, I WILL TAKE THE FOLLOWING
THREE ACTIONS TO SAVE MONEY:

1. _____

2. _____

3. _____

TOTAL SAVINGS FROM EXERCISE:

$ _____

FIND YOUR POWER— GIVE TO OTHERS

The secret to life is to become a
"go giver"—not a "go getter"
~ Sir John Templeton

Congratulations! You have come a long way on your journey to Starting Over and Finishing Rich. In truth, these ten steps have been about more than just money. They are about putting you back in touch with your personal power. By taking action, you are acting out your belief in the possibility of a rich life—one filled with less worry, less doubt, and more courage for you and your family.

There is another way to feel your power to make a difference in your own life—you can make a difference in the lives of others. Over the years, I have seen firsthand that nothing shifts our focus from doubt and worry to courage and strength faster than doing what we can do to better the world and help others.

BE A HERO IN THIS STORY

Right now you may be thinking, "David, I'm reading this book because I'm worried about my financial future! How can I possibly think about giving anything away when I'm trying to start over?" This is a completely understandable reaction. But consider this: Within each and every one of us lies the power to not only change our own destinies but to change the destinies of others less fortunate than us. If you want to truly believe one, you must truly believe the other.

Back in Step 1, I wrote about the human spirit. It's the force we all possess that drives us to overcome adversity and live extraordinary lives. I'm betting that *your* spirit is strong, determined, resilient, and smart. Why? Because if it weren't, you would have never picked up this book.

The world needs people like you, people with the "right stuff" who can be the heroes in the economic drama that's been playing out on the world stage for the past year or two. Sure, we've all been hurt by the recession, but some of us have been hurt far worse than others. Are there people you know—neighbors, friends, family—who are worse off than you? I'm willing to bet there are.

My point is not to make you feel guilty but to get you to realize the amazing opportunity you have. John D. Rockefeller, one of the all-time greatest philanthropists, once said, "Think of giving not as a duty but as a privilege." The opportunity to make a difference in the lives of our fellow humans is a privilege for certain. It is also a great way to attract more happiness and opportunity into your life.

DECIDE WHAT YOU CAN GIVE AND MAKE IT AUTOMATIC

So decide today that you're going to give back a percentage of your income in order to help others less fortunate than you. You'll be in good company. According to a study by the Giving USA Foundation, despite the recession Americans donated nearly $309 billion to charity in 2008. That was a higher level of giving than in any year on record except for 2007. And it wasn't a fluke. In January 2009, Cygnus Applied Research surveyed more than 17,000 charitable donors and found that the majority had no intention of cutting back their level of giving in 2009.

What this demonstrates is that even in the middle of a recession we Americans can be amazingly generous.

How much should you give? That's completely up to you. It might be 10%; it might be 1%. Give what you can afford to give. If you're not sure, start small and aim to increase your charitable giving over time. Perhaps as you make progress on your own road to financial recovery, you'll be able to increase the amount you give.

Giving back works best when you make a consistent commitment. The key is to put aside a set percentage of your income every time you get paid. If you wait until the end of the year to see what is "left over," you will almost certainly wind up donating less—maybe even nothing. So my advice is to make your donations automatic by arranging to have a percentage of your income automatically deducted from your paycheck or checking account and transferred to the charity of your choice.

WHAT CAUSES SPEAK TO YOUR HEART?

Support a cause that truly means something to you. If you don't have a favorite charity, consider giving to an organization that's working to meet the basic needs of the people hardest hit by the recession—for example, a local food bank, church, synagogue, or homeless shelter. You might also consider well-known charities like the United Way (**www.unitedway.org**), Goodwill (www.goodwill.org), and the Salvation Army (**www. salvationarmy.org**), all of which see a big increase in demand for their services during tough economic times.

Whatever you decide to do, you want to make sure you are giving to a reputable charity. What makes a charity reputable? One sure sign is not running up big administrative expenses but actually spending the vast bulk of the money it collects on the people or causes it is supposed to be supporting. Most experts agree that a charity should pass through at least 70% to 75% of what it raises—meaning its administrative expenses should never exceed 25%.

I personally never give money to any charity until I've had a chance to look at its financial records. If you're going to give money to an organization, you deserve to know how the organization is going to spend it. So ask to see the financials and make a point of finding out what percentage of the money raised actually goes to the people the charity claims to be helping. If a charity won't show you its records, find one that will.

FIGURING OUT WHO DESERVES YOUR SUPPORT

There is no end to the great resources on the Internet that will help you figure out what groups deserve your support. Here are a few of my favorites:

www.justgive.org

JustGive is a great place to start, providing links to more than one million public charities, including complete reports and financial records. Designed to help you identify the charities that are most meaningful to *you*, this user-friendly website can process donations for you, and if you register, it can also help you keep track of all your contributions.

www.bbb.org/charity

The website of the Better Business Bureau Wise Giving Alliance, this used to be known as Give.org. It collects and distributes information on countless nonprofit organizations that solicit nationally or have national or international program services. It also certifies charities that meet its Standards for Charity Accountability as "BBB Accredited Charities." So before you make any donations, be smart and check out what this site has to say about the organizations you may be considering.

www.guidestar.org

Formed in 1994, Guidestar aims to assist responsible giving by providing the kind of due diligence would-be philanthropists know they should do but don't always have time for. Its website is loaded with solid and helpful data, including a database of more than a million nonprofit organizations.

www.charitynavigator.org
Billing itself as "Your Guide to Intelligent Giving,"
Charity Navigator claims to be the nation's largest
and most-utilized evaluator of charities, focusing on
the financial health of more than 5,000 well-known
charities. The Top 10 lists featured on their home
page are worth a look.

www.networkforgood.org
This site is a good solution for one-stop charity
shopping. It allows you not only to research any of
1.5 million charities, but also to make secure donations to any of them online. Network for Good also
helps you keep your tax records up to date by storing
your donation history, and it allows you to save lists
of your favorite charities.

SOME OF MY FAVORITE CHARITIES

Over the years, I've dedicated part of the royalties of
many of my books to different charities.

The Automatic Millionaire Homeowner inspired
me to give to Habitat for Humanity New York
(**www.habitatnyc.org**). What started as a one-day
outing to work on a home in the Bronx with my team
and a group of FinishRich readers led us to sponsor a
building that eight families now call home. I have
since joined their board of directors.

I dedicated royalties from *Go Green, Live Rich* to the Waterkeeper Alliance (**www.waterkeeper.org**), a grassroots advocacy organization dedicated to preserving and protecting our waterways from polluters. Founded in 1999 by environmental attorney and activist Robert F. Kennedy, Jr., Waterkeeper Alliance is a global movement of nearly 200 local Waterkeeper organizations who patrol and protect more than 100,000 miles of rivers, streams, and coastlines in North and South America, Europe, Australia, Asia, and Africa.

Smart Women Finish Rich inspired me to join my close friends on the board of directors of a charity called Makers of Memories (**www.makersof memories.org**). It provides battered mothers and their children who have witnessed domestic violence in their homes with financial resources to enjoy their very first vacation, so they can form memories that will change their lives forever. (So far, we've gone on a cruise and a trip to Disneyland.)

This book is dedicated to **www.charitywater .com**. Founded by Scott Harrison in 2006, charity: water is a nonprofit organization that brings clean, safe drinking water to people in developing nations. Through proceeds from *Start Over, Finish Rich*, we will be funding a water well in Africa.

I share all this with you not to brag but to provide an example of how you can choose a cause you care about and get involved with both your time and your money. It's not always easy to make the effort, but I keep doing it because ultimately I know it matters. And, candidly, in the end it always feels good!

ANOTHER WAY TO GIVE— VOLUNTEERING TIME AND TALENT INSTEAD OF MONEY

If it's simply not possible right now for you to give money to a charity, then consider donating some time. Rolling up your sleeves and getting involved can give you even greater joy—and most charities could certainly use the help! I've never come across a charitable organization that couldn't use committed volunteers willing to donate their time and talent to help others. In fact, donating your time can often be more useful than donating your money. And for the giver, donating time can be incredibly meaningful. I've given both money and time to charities, and the experience of giving my time has had far more of an impact on my life than the experience of writing checks.

Here are some great websites that can help you get started volunteering your time to help others.

www.volunteermatch.org
Volunteer Match is a nonprofit service that will match your individual interests, location, and schedule with community-service opportunities in your area. More than 68,000 nonprofit organizations use

this service to recruit volunteers, so check it out to find opportunities in your area.

www.idealist.org

This is the website for Action Without Borders, a service dedicated to connecting people, organizations, and resources to "help build a world where all people can live free and dignified lives." Their site will enable you to search opportunities with more than 84,000 nonprofit organizations in more than 180 countries.

www.charities.org

America's Charities have distributed more than $400 million to more than 4,000 charities since 1980 through workplace giving campaigns. Visit this site to find out how your company can sponsor a charitable campaign for employees.

www.nationalservice.org

The Corporation for National and Community Service provides opportunities for Americans of all ages and backgrounds to serve at the national, state, or city level. Research a wide variety of government programs, including those offered by Americorps, Senior Corps, and Learn and Serve America.

www.nvoad.org

The National Voluntary Organizations Active in Disaster coordinates planning efforts by many voluntary organizations that are involved in responding to disasters. Click on the "Members" tab to find out how you can get involved.

www.mentoring.org

The National Mentoring Partnership is a resource for mentors and mentoring initiatives nationwide. Its website allows you to explore available mentoring opportunities and to sign up for online training to become a better mentor.

www.score.org

SCORE, which stands for Service Corps of Retired Executives, describes itself as "Counselors to America's Small Business." What it does is provide entrepreneurs with free, confidential business counseling. If you want to share your business expertise and give back to your community, you might consider volunteering your services to SCORE.

DON'T FORGET YOUR TAX BREAK!

People will tell you that the great thing about charitable contributions is that they allow you to do good *and* reduce your income-tax bill at the same time. But be careful—not all charitable donations are tax-deductible.

In order to be able to deduct a charitable contribution from your taxable income, the recipient of your donation must be qualified by the IRS as a 501(c)(3) organization. To find out if the charity you want to support is one, ask them. To make doubly sure, visit the IRS website and check IRS Publication 78, which lists qualified organizations. You can also call the IRS toll-free at (877) 829-5500.

The rules regarding cash donations to qualified charities are pretty straightforward. Basically, all you need to do is keep copies of canceled checks or other receipts. The rules regarding donations of goods or services are a bit more complicated, and for the most part you can forget about trying to get a deduction for any time you donate (no matter how valuable you might think your time is). IRS Publication 526, "Charitable Giving," lays out all the rules concerning charitable donations, and to be on the safe side, you might want to download it from the IRS website (www.irs.gov).

GIVE AND YOU SHALL RECEIVE

It's tempting to think of this step as something optional that you don't really have to do in order to start over and finish rich. That's not how I see it.

Over nearly two decades of working as a financial coach for thousands of people, I've witnessed time and time again that the fastest way to feel rich is to give more—and that those who give more become rich faster. I don't think it's a coincidence. Research shows definitively that people who give of their time and money to help others live longer, happier, and wealthier lives.

So go with the flow of the universe. Follow this basic law of nature and your journey on the road to financial recovery will be that much quicker and more joyful.

TO DO IN 2010 ✔

☐ To truly feel your power to make a difference, decide to give what you can, no matter how little.

☐ Choose a cause you believe in at www.justgive.org.

☐ Make your contributions automatic by scheduling regular deductions from your checking account, paid to the charity of your choice.

A FINAL WORD: MY PERSONAL "START OVER" STORY

At the beginning of this book, I told you we would be collecting stories on the FinishRich website (**www. FinishRich.com**) and our Facebook page (**www.facebook.com/DavidBach**) from people who have started over. Hopefully, you will share your story soon! I believe it's important to collect these stories because I know nothing helps conquer fear or despair more than hearing about other people with lives like ours who have overcome hardship and moved forward to a stronger and better life. Speaking personally, whenever I read about someone who has done something I want to do, it gives me strength, because I think, "If they can do it, so can I."

IF IT HAS BEEN DONE BEFORE, IT CAN BE DONE AGAIN

In his classic book *Think and Grow Rich*, Napoleon Hill says something that I think is incredibly important: "IF IT HAS BEEN DONE BEFORE, IT CAN BE DONE AGAIN."

That is one of life's greatest truths. Wherever you are now, and wherever you want to go, I promise you—someone else has made that journey, and you can make it too.

It is in this spirit that I want to share my personal "Start Over" story. It is my story of overcoming adversity. It hasn't been easy, but I am starting over—and life is getting better each and every day. And if I can do it, so can you!

HITTING MY OWN "RESET BUTTON"

Back in January of 2007, I made a decision that would force me to "start over" my whole life. The brutal decision I made was to get divorced. It was not a decision I took lightly, and it is not one I am proud of having had to make, much less share. Michelle and I met in 1993, and we had been married for nearly ten years. Unfortunately, our marriage had lost its way, as so many often do, and after years of struggling to make it work, we both had reached the point where we were tired of trying.

Both of us came from families where everyone got married and stayed married. Divorce just wasn't in our background. But while neither of us wanted to be divorced, neither could we figure out how to get back to where we once had been. It was heartbreaking and sad and difficult—all the more so because we had a young child, our son Jack, who had just turned three.

When you get divorced, you wind up reevaluating everything in your life. We started off with great intentions and a commitment to put Jack first. We both wanted to make our separation as easy and painless as we could, but in reality it was really tough. Negotiating the details of child custody and dividing our assets while simultaneously trying to rebuild our lives as single parents took a toll on us both. The pain and fear and uncertainty of our respective futures complicated every decision we were making. Two years later we were still unsettled, and by the beginning of 2009, I had pretty much given up. I was ready to accept that we simply couldn't come to an agreement and would have no choice but to fight it out in court (which neither of us truly wanted). My attorney warned me that going to court would prolong the process for at least another year—maybe two—and I could look forward to our legal bill doubling.

After two sleepless nights, I stumbled into my office, delirious from worry and exhaustion, with the intention of making a decision. My office was piled high with file boxes and binders filled with documents related to my divorce—legal notices, emails, asset valuations, notes from meetings. It was simply brutal. As often happens, my divorce had become a full-time job. And worst of all, I had reached a point where all the tools I had taught and previously used to live a great life were no longer working for me. I was frozen with worry, sick with the realization of having failed at marriage, concerned about Jack and how he would be affected by our divorce, and anxious about losing a lot of money.

GETTING GRATEFUL—
HOW I STARTED OVER

And then I did something that turned my life around. It was something I had been teaching my students and readers to do for years. I opened up my journal and made a gratitude list.

For more than six hours, I wrote down everything in my life that was working, everything I had to be grateful for—starting with my son, Jack. I wrote about my family and friends and their love and support over the years. I wrote about the good times Michelle and I had shared, the respect we had for each other and the love we still shared for our son. I wrote about my life's journey and my life's work, and what I had accomplished. I wrote about my assets— not my money, but my real assets: what I had contributed to the world around me and what I hoped to contribute in the future.

As I read over my list, I came to the unstoppable realization that who I was, the person I had become over the last 13 years of my marriage, couldn't be divided by lawyers or courts. My money and property could be split up, but who I was as a person was, as it says in the Pledge of Allegiance, indivisible. Most important, the incredible heartache we both had in our hearts would someday heal.

I could re-earn the money I would lose in the divorce. I could reestablish my business and buy a new home. I could rebuild my retirement savings. I could be the ultimate father, even if it meant being a single father. I could survive this.

Sitting in my office after six hours of writing, I realized that my life could START OVER—and I could THRIVE AGAIN. So could Michelle.

So I called my divorce attorney—whom I had told two days earlier to "get me a court date"—and I said, "Let's schedule a meeting and settle this." I then called Michelle and said, "Please let's get in a room and settle this," and she said, "I agree. Let's do it!"

I REPRIORITIZED MY WHOLE LIFE

As I write this, less than a year has passed since I sat in my office writing my gratitude list. Amazingly enough, Michelle and Jack and I are all happier than we've probably been in at least five years. Michelle and I have both moved on to other relationships, and now get along so well that many people who see us together at Jack's school don't realize we are divorced. And Jack himself is doing incredibly well, sharing two homes with two parents who love him and appreciate every day we have with him.

I'm not sure I would have ever believed that my life could fall so far so fast in such a short period—nor that it could recover and be so much better and stronger so quickly. Because of the pain I've been through, I believe I'm a better person. I have grown, become more compassionate, and am a better dad. Today, I have Jack half of the time, and when he's with me, he comes first. I take him to and from school (this year I was the "class mom"), attend his after-school events, and just spend a ton of time hanging out with him.

In short, I have reprioritized my whole life. I don't expect it to always be this good—but I will tell you that I am truly living rich and I am truly grateful.

Now here's the most important point of all: This all came about because I made a decision to "start over." I don't recommend divorce—that's not the point of this story. My point is that the journey of falling down and getting up again happens to ALL OF US. And the fruit of life, the true blessings, often come when we get back up again.

So if you have fallen down—if the recession we just lived through has thrown you for a loop, if you have lost a job or a loved one, or if you are stuck right now in a life you are not happy with—please trust me, my friend, and believe me when I say you can get back up again. You can be stronger, you can be happier and more grateful, than you were before.

Whatever you may have lost in the last few years—that's behind you. If it was money, you can go make more and rebuild. What's more important is the love you have inside you, for it is what will get you through the tough times. All you need to do is focus on what's working and be grateful for it. And if you feel stuck, do what I did. Pull out a pad and start writing down what you have to be grateful for. Focus on what you have done with your life that is positive and special—most important of all, the people you have loved and loved you. None of that can be taken from you—not by a recession, not by a lost job, not by a divorce.

Life is too short to stay down. So please take this

book—take your dreams—and START OVER. I'm doing it today—and you can, too! I know you can.

Thank you for reading this book, and please know that I am honored and grateful that you spent this time with me. I hope to meet you someday along this amazing journey. You can reach me at www.finishrich.com and www.facebook.com/DavidBach.

You can also send me an email directly and share your story at success@finishrich.com. While I can't promise you a personal response, please know that I try to read every email that comes my way. It is readers like you who inspire me to keep doing what I do.

God bless you—now go get started!

Your friend,
David Bach
Sag Harbor, N.Y.
August 2009

ACKNOWLEDGMENTS

It's almost impossible for me to believe that we are putting my eleventh book to bed. There are now more than 7 million copies of the books in the FinishRich Series around the world.

What started as a dream to help one million women become smarter with their money—with *Smart Women Finish Rich* back in 1998—has become a full-time calling for me, with every day dedicated to financial literacy and the empowerment of millions around the world.

So I want to start with a deep and meaningful thank-you to YOU, the readers of my books. It is YOU who have kept me on this path. It is YOU who have taken the time to read my books, stop me in airports or on the street, and tell me what my books have meant to you. It is YOU who have emailed me over the years to share your success stories—and let me know what's working and not working. I know that not everyone who reads a book writes to the author—so I have truly been blessed to have received thousands and thousands of "thank-you" emails and letters over the last decade. And I must say, some days it is those letters alone that keep me going. Because what makes all the hard work worth it is when I hear from you that what I'm doing is helping you.

So to YOU—for reading this book (and maybe some of my previous books, too)—thank you for your trust in me and for your continued encouragement.

To my team at Broadway Books, a profound thank-you. The past year was a tough one in the book business—and as we head into 2010, I'm grateful to continue to have the support of such a talented and dedicated team: Kristine Puopolo, David Drake, Diane Salvatore, Jenny Frost, Rachel Rokicki, Catherine Pollock, Whitney Cookman, Stephanie Bowen, Chris Fortunato, Peter Grennen, and Adam Bohannon.

To Allan Mayer and Liz Dougherty, "Thank you—we did it again" seems so small, but we *did* do it again and I am truly proud of us for pulling it off. I couldn't have done it without you—YOU ARE TRULY A DREAM TEAM. To Elisa Garafano, thank you for keeping the office running while I was off writing.

To Suzanne Gluck and Jay Mandel, thank you as always for your agency's brilliance and guidance. Here's to many more successes together!

To Stephen Breimer, as always, you are an invaluable friend, partner, and protector in this and all my business dealings. Thank you for always being there on a moment's notice.

To my son, Jack Bach—buddy, I love you so much it's just ridiculous. You are the best thing that ever happened to me. Nothing else compares to how much I love you—and how happy you make me and how proud of you I am. Thanks for listening to me at dinner as I negotiated this book deal and then providing me with a five-year-old's guidance. You are truly "Yoda."

To Alatia—I love you so much and I am so grateful every day that you have come into our lives. Thank you for saying "yes" and for changing my life and making it all better.

To Michelle—thank you for being the best "ex" a guy could ask for. I know it's bizarre to the rest of the world how well we get along, but I am grateful we do—and I will always love you and want the best for you. To Joan and Bill, thank you for being so great during the past few years as we took the path we did. You will always be family to me. And to Gene, thank you for making Michelle so happy—and for loving Jack so much. Thank you also to Connie Nji, for loving and taking such amazing care of Jack and me. I am grateful every day that you came into our lives to be Jack's nanny.

To my parents—I love you so much! Thank you for always loving me and supporting me—you truly are the best parents.

To my sister Emily and brother-in-law Tom, I love you and miss you and wish we weren't living 3,000 miles apart.

Finally, to my dear friends Tom Cooper, David Rich, Brian Martin, Roark Dunn, Andrew Donner, David Kronick, Drew Warmington, Adam Young, and Nicola Zahn—you have been my bedrock through both the tough times and the good times. Thank you! I really love you and feel grateful to have such great friends.

David Bach

Sag Harbor, N.Y.

August 2009

INDEX

ABOUT THE AUTHOR

David Bach has helped millions of people around the world take action to live and finish rich. He is one of the most popular and prolific financial authors of our time, with nine consecutive national bestsellers, including two consecutive #1 *New York Times* bestsellers, *Start Late, Finish Rich* and *The Automatic Millionaire*, as well as the national and international bestsellers *Fight for Your Money*; *Go Green, Live Rich*; *The Automatic Millionaire Homeowner*; *Smart Women Finish Rich*; *Smart Couples Finish Rich*; *The Finish Rich Workbook*; and *The Automatic Millionaire Workbook*. Bach carries the unique distinction of having had four of his books appear simultaneously on the *Wall Street Journal*, *BusinessWeek*, and *USA Today* bestseller lists. In addition, four of Bach's books were named to *USA Today*'s Best Sellers of the Year list for 2004. In all, his FinishRich Books have been published in more than 15 languages, with more than 7 million copies in print worldwide.

Bach's breakout book, *The Automatic Millionaire*, was the #1 business book of 2004, according to *BusinessWeek*. It spent 14 weeks on the *New York Times* bestseller list and was simultaneously number one on the bestseller lists of the *New York Times*, *BusinessWeek*, *USA Today*, and the *Wall Street Journal*. With more than a million copies in print, this simple and powerful book has been translated into 12 languages and has inspired thousands around the world to save money automatically.

Bach is regularly featured in the media. He has appeared six times on *The Oprah Winfrey Show* to share his strategies for living and finishing rich and has made regular appearances on NBC's *Today* and *Weekend Today* shows, CNN's *Larry King Live*, ABC's *Live with Regis and Kelly*, *The View*, CBS's *Early Show*, ABC News, Fox News, and CNBC. He has been profiled in many major publications, including the *New*

York Times, BusinessWeek, USA Today, People, Reader's Digest, Time, Financial Times, the *Washington Post,* the *Wall Street Journal,* the *Los Angeles Times,* the *San Francisco Chronicle, Working Woman, Glamour, Family Circle,* and *Redbook.* He has been a contributor to *Redbook* magazine, *Smart Money* magazine, Yahoo! Finance, and AOL Money. In 2009, Bach was a regular on the *Today* show "Money 911" segments and a contributor to ABC's *Good Money.*

David Bach is the creator of the FinishRich® Seminar series, which highlights his quick and easy-to-follow financial strategies. In just the last few years, more than half a million people have learned how to take financial action to live a life in line with their values by attending his Smart Women Finish Rich®, Smart Couples Finish Rich®, and Find the Money Seminars, which have been taught in more than 2,000 cities throughout North America by thousands of financial advisors.

A renowned motivational and financial speaker, Bach regularly presents seminars for and delivers keynote addresses to the world's leading financial service firms, Fortune 500 companies, universities, and national conferences. He is the founder and chairman of FinishRich Media, a company dedicated to revolutionizing the way people learn about money. Prior to founding FinishRich Media, he was a senior vice president of Morgan Stanley and a partner of The Bach Group, which during his tenure (1993 to 2001) managed more than half a billion dollars for individual investors.

As part of his mission, David Bach is involved with many worthwhile causes, including serving on the board of Habitat for Humanity New York and cofounding Makers of Memories, a charity organization dedicated to helping women and children who are victims of domestic violence.

David Bach lives in New York. Please visit his website at www.finishrich.com.

David Bach is donating $1 for each copy of *Start Over, Finish Rich* that is sold in 2010 (up to $20,000) to charity: water, a nonprofit organization bringing clean and safe drinking water to people in developing nations. This donation will go toward sponsoring a freshwater well and latrines at a school and will serve over 1,000 students.

One hundred percent of public donations go directly to projects on the ground. Through the help of more than 60,000 donors worldwide, in just three years charity: water has raised $11 million and brought clean water to over 700,000 people in 16 countries. To make a donation, visit their website at **www.charitywater.org**.